WORLD OF WALLS

World of Walls

The Structure, Roles and Effectiveness of Separation Barriers

Said Saddiki

OpenBook Publishers

ISBN Paperback: 978-1-78374-368-1
ISBN Hardback: 978-1-78374-369-8
ISBN Digital (PDF): 978-1-78374-370-4
ISBN Digital ebook (epub): 978-1-78374-371-1
ISBN Digital ebook (mobi): 978-1-78374-372-8
DOI: 10.11647/OBP.0121

Cover image: Ted Eytan, *Sunset at the White House* (2017), CC BY-SA 2.0, Flickr, https://www.flickr.com/photos/taedc/32722159326
Cover design: Anna Gatti

All paper used by Open Book Publishers is SFI (Sustainable Forestry Initiative), PEFC (Programme for the Endorsement of Forest Certification Schemes) and Forest Stewardship Council(r)(FSC(r) certified.

Printed in the United Kingdom, United States, and Australia
by Lightning Source for Open Book Publishers (Cambridge, UK)

Contents

Introduction

In the past physical walls and fences surrounding territorial space, towns and villages were viewed by ancient nations from a defensive perspective, as a fortification to defend their territorial sovereignty and a rampart to protect themselves from the outside attacks. Dramatic changes in both military doctrine and technology in the last century led to a decline in the strategic and tactic importance of borders as a line of defense. Although one of the key aspects of the traditional notion of sovereignty was the right for states to control exclusively the movement of people across territorial boundaries and to expel undesirable aliens and immigrants, nowadays this authority has come into question not only because of increased globalization, but also because of great intellectual efforts to re-theorize the notion of the nation-state and its components, including the concepts of sovereignty and national borders.

The means and systems used in border control developed throughout history have depended on the evolution of the military and security industries. In recent decades, border-control systems have developed dramatically along with a rapid growth of both authorized and unauthorized cross-border activities, including the flow of people, goods, ideas, drug, weapons, capital and information. This increase in physical-border barriers contradicts the trend for some globalist and trans-national perspectives that envisage a "Borderless World", "A World without Sovereignty", "The End of Geography", "The End of the Nation-State" and so on.

Although the construction of border barriers has confirmed security concerns and strengthened the position of sovereign states as realists have emphasized, transnational non-state actors — the primary group

 https://doi.org/10.11647/OBP.0121.01

these walls and fences were erected to exclude — have seriously questioned state-centered theories. The gap between theory and practice has widened enormously after 9/11, when transnational non-state actors, or what Peter Andreas has termed "clandestine transnational actors",[1] became not only the main rival of nation states but also a major threat to security, whereas interstate wars have declined steadily since the beginning of the third millennium.

At the same time, globalists have announced that the territorial border is going to become progressively blurred and eroded due to the combined pressures of the growing presence of transnational non-state actors and the interactions between globalization and information and communication technologies (ICTs), a sphere often theorized in terms of virtualization of trans-border and trans-national flows. James Rosenau has argued that this shift in perception occurring in the post-Cold War era is "diminishing the competence and effectiveness of states and rendering their borders more porous and less meaningful".[2] In a similar vein, Kenichi Ohmae, in his well-known book *The Borderless World*, confidently announced that "while everyone living on this earth is to one degree or another already living in an interlinked economy, at the same time, we all continue moving further toward the reality of a world without border".[3] In contrast, Saskia Sassen notes that, despite a growing consensus among developed countries to facilitate the flow of goods, information, and capital, when it comes to regulating the movement of people, "the national state claims its old splendor in asserting its sovereign right to control its borders".[4] Although globalization has diminished the traditional military and economic functions of borders,

---

1   Peter Andreas defines "clandestine transnational actors" (CTAs) "as non-state actors who operate across national borders in violation of state laws and who attempt to evade law enforcement efforts". Peter Andreas, "Redrawing the Line: Borders and Security in the Twenty-First Century", *International Security*, Vol. 28, No. 2 (2003), p. 78.
2   James N. Rosenau, "New Dimensions of Security: The Interaction of Globalizing the Localizing Dynamics", *Security Dialogue*, Vol. 25, No. 3 (1994), p. 258.
3   Kenichi Ohmae, *The Borderless World: Power and Strategy in the Interlinked Economy*. New York: Harper Business, 1999, p. xiv.
4   Saskia Sassen, *Losing Control? Sovereignty in an Age of Globalization*. New York: Columbia University Press, 1996, p. 59.

it has also created more border-policing work for nation-states[5] which now spend millions of dollars annually to fortify their national borders.

Anna Feigenbaum identified what she called "globalized fences" by four commonalities: first, they serve transnational security functions, particularly in the post-9/11 era, when transnational actors are perceived to have become the greatest threat to the nation-state. Second, they are contracted through multinational companies. Third, they are built with materials imported from different nations. Finally, they integrate 'virtual' and physical technologies. Advanced digital and virtual technologies work in conjunction with human patrols, communications devices and physical barriers.[6]

The growth of the walls has taken different paths in the post-World War II period.[7] Only nineteen walls and barriers were built between 1945 and 1991, and seven walls were added between 1991 and 2001 to the thirteen that survived the Cold War. The erection of border walls pauses briefly after the Cold War, but the post-9/11 period has seen the return of the wall as a political object and instrument.[8] Twenty-eight walls have been erected or planned in the post-9/11 period.

Modern international barriers are defined according to their specific contexts and functions which are reflected in their various designations: security, military, defensive or anti-terror wall; fence or barrier and so on. Opponents of such walled borders adopt their own terminology which reflects how they perceive these barriers. Separation, shame, apartheid, or political/ideological walls are widely used to criticize fencing policies.

These barriers reflect the economic disparity between countries in many levels. Firstly, building states are significantly richer than target

---

5   Peter Andreas, "Redrawing the Line", p. 84.

6   Anna Feigenbaum, "Concrete Needs no Metaphor: Globalized Fences as Sites of Political Struggle", *Ephemera*, Vol. 10, No. 2 (2010), pp. 121–23.

7   Élisabeth Vallet and Charles-Philippe David, "Introduction. Du retour des murs frontaliers en relations internationales", *Études internationales*, Vol. 43, No. 1 (2012), pp. 5–25 ; Élisabeth Vallet, "Toujours plus de murs dans un monde sans frontières", *Le Devoir* (26 October 2009), http://www.ledevoir.com/international/actualites-internationales/273594/toujours-plus-de-murs-dans-un-monde-sans-frontieres; Vallet and David "The (Re)Building of the Wall in International Relations", *Journal of Borderlands Studies*, Vol. 27, No. 2 (2012), pp. 111–19.

8   *Ibid.*, p. 113.

states.[9] Secondly, some border barriers (U.S.-Mexico barrier and Spanish fences in northern Morocco) embody what is called the "frontier of poverty"[10] or "The Great Wall of Capital"[11] that dramatically separate the global rich from the rest of the world. Thirdly, a large number of these border barriers were built to prevent irregular immigration from lesser-developed countries. On the two sides of the wall, there is always a significant potential imbalance of power, as well as asymmetric confidence.[12] Walls are never built against an equivalent power. When the targeted country is considered reliable, the fortification of the common border is adopted bilaterally. For example, the government of the United States collaborates extensively with Canada to control its northern border, while it imposes a border fence with Mexico.[13]

The current border barriers can be sorted geographically. Asia, as the most fenced continent, contains almost twenty border barriers: India-Pakistan; India-Bangladesh; India-Myanmar; Pakistan-Afghanistan; Myanmar-Bangladesh; Iran-Pakistan; Iran-Afghanistan; Kazakhstan-Uzbekistan; China-North Korea; Malaysia-Thailand; Uzbekistan-Afghanistan; Turkmenistan-Uzbekistan; Uzbekistan-Kirgizstan; Brunei-eastern Malaysia (Limbang); South Korea-North Korea. In the Middle East, Israel has fenced off its entire *de facto* border with Palestinians and Arab countries adjacent to Palestine. In the Gulf, because of security and immigration reasons, most of the countries of the region, especially Saudi Arabia, have tried to fortify their borders: Israel-West Bank; Israel-Gaza Strip; Israel-Egypt; Israel-Jordan; Israel-Lebanon; Israel-Syria; Turkey-Syria, Egypt-Gaza Strip; Saudi Arabia-Yemen; Saudi Arabia-Iraq; Saudi Arabia-Oman; Saudi Arabia-Qatar; Saudi Arabia-United Arab Emirates; United Arab Emirates-Oman; Jordan-Iraq; Kuwait-Iraq.

---

9   Ron Hassner and Jason Wittenberg, "Barriers to Entry: Who Builds Fortified Boundaries and Are They Likely to Work?", Paper presented at the annual meeting of the American Political Science Association, Toronto, Canada (3–6 September 2009).

10   Roland Freudenstein, "Rio Odra, Rio Buh: Poland, Germany, and the Borders of Twenty-First-Century Europe", in *The Wall Around the West: State Borders and Immigration Controls in North America and Europe*, Peter Andreas and Timothy Snyder (Eds.). Oxford: Rowman and Littlefield, 2000, p. 174.

11   Mike Davis, "The Great Wall of Capital", in *Border Culture*. Ilan Stavans (Ed.). Santa Barbara: Greenwood, 2009, p. 27.

12   Évelyne Ritaine, "La barrière et le checkpoint: Mise en politique de l'asymétrie", *Cultures & Conflits*, No. 73 (2009), p. 21.

13   *Ibid.*, p. 20.

In Africa, there are more than eight border barriers: Morocco wall in Western Sahara; Spain-Morocco (Ceuta); Spain-Morocco (Melilla); South Africa-Mozambique; South Africa-Zimbabwe; Zimbabwe-Zambia, Botswana-Zimbabwe; Mozambique-Zambia. Europe, because of the advanced regional integration process, has not witnessed a growth in border walls after the end of the Cold War. Instead, separating walls in Europe have been dismantled (e.g., the Berlin wall and the Belfast wall). Today, there are only a few physical border barriers in Europe: Greek-Turkish Cyprus; Russia (Abkhazia)-Georgia; Gibraltar-Spain; Hungary-Serbia; Hungary-Croatia, although some new ones have been built in recent times in response to the refugee 'crisis'. In North America, because of irregular immigration flows, the United States fenced off its borders with Mexico and Canada. Latin America is almost free of physical-border barriers except for those erected by the U.S. between Guantanamo and Cuba.

The growth in border barriers all over the world has created a huge security business. Private companies account for the bulk of this growing market. The major armament and defense companies are at the heart of the border-security market, but firms specializing in communications, surveillance, information technology or biometrics also take a significant part in this new multi-billion-dollar market.[14] Israeli companies are the most famous in this area. Since 2002, exports of Israeli technology in border security services increased by 22 percent each year, and there are about 450 Israeli companies specializing in securing territory.[15] The major international companies that claim the lion share of this market include *Boeing* (American multinational aerospace and defense corporation), *Elbit Systems* (Israeli defense electronics manufacturers and integrators), *Magal Security Systems* (Israeli company operating in more than 75 countries worldwide), *Amper* (Spanish multinational group), *Indra Sistemas* (Spanish information technology and defense company) and *EADS Group* (European Aeronautic Defense and Space Company).

---

14   Julien Saada, "L'économie du mur: Un marché en pleine expansion", *Le Devoir* (27 October 2009), http://www.ledevoir.com/international/actualites-internationales/271687/l-economie-du-mur-un-marche-en-pleine-expansion

15   *Ibid.*

Even if their primary objective is to secure the border, physical barriers are seen by some targeted countries as a unilateral attempt to demarcate common borders, especially when it comes to occupied or disputed territories that can be turned to *de facto* boundaries (e.g., the Israeli barriers, the fences of Ceuta and Melilla, the Indian fence in Kashmir, the India-Bangladesh border and the Uzbekistan-Kyrgyzstan border). So, although in some cases it can be argued that the reinforcement of a nation-state's borders is based on security requirements, recent history has demonstrated that states hide their real goals behind security issues. Since almost all border barriers are erected by unilateral decision — with few exceptions (e.g., the U.S.-Canada border and the Malaysia-Thailand Border), they are always disputed, even when they are built on a national boundary or on private property.[16] Targeted countries always emphasize that border-security policies should be bilateral and a result of cooperation.

This book consists of five chapters. The first, "Israel and the Fencing Policy", examines aspects of various separation barriers built by Israel since its inception in 1948 and evaluates their effectiveness in order to show whether such a policy makes Israel more secure.

The second chapter, "Border Fencing in India", provides an overview of the complicated characteristics of India's borders with adjacent countries and deals with the Indian strategy of fencing borders with some of its neighbors. Despite the diversity of India's border-fencing projects, security concerns are the top priority of the border-control systems.

The third chapter, "The Fences of Ceuta and Melilla", investigates the controversial aspects of Ceuta and Melilla's fences as the EU southern border and highlights the changing roles of the two enclaves' fences. The barriers of Ceuta and Melilla provide a fitting model to examine the gap between governments' stated purposes and hidden objectives.

The fourth chapter, "The U.S.-Mexico Border Wall", analyzes the relationship between the U.S. immigration policy and border-control systems at a time when militarizing and fencing of the southern border remain the cornerstone of the U.S. strategy to keep unwanted immigrants out of its territory.

---

16   Évelyne Ritaine, "La barrière et le checkpoint: Mise en politique de l'asymétrie", p. 21.

The last chapter, "The Wall of Western Sahara", focuses on the military wall built by Morocco in Western Sahara. The chapter presents the status and prospects of the Sahara sand wall (or "berm"), as well as a glance at the Western Sahara issue. Although the Sahara wall was built, at first, in a specific context and for a specific military goal, today it embodies the lingering disputes arising from a long-term and ongoing conflict — the Western Sahara issue that continues to threaten the stability of the Maghreb region.

1. Israel and the Fencing Policy[1]

Since its inception in 1948, Israel has established barriers of varying structures and effectiveness between populations of Jewish Israelis and their Arab neighbors. This policy has been a constant element of Israel's security doctrine, rooted in Zionist thought from its beginning.[2] Writing of Palestine, the father of modern political Zionism, Theodor Herzl remarked in his book *The Jewish State*,[3] that "we should there form a portion of the rampart of Europe against Asia, an outpost of civilization as opposed to barbarism".[4] Uri Avnery, an Israeli peace activist and journalist, argues that, more than a hundred years later, Ariel Sharon's wall expresses exactly the same outlook; separating its "civilization" from "others".[5] The idea of building a separation wall in Palestine dates back to 1923, when Ze'ev Jabotinsky, one of the most influential Zionist leaders and the ideological father of today's Likud Party, published two essays entitled "The Iron Wall: Israel and the Arab

---

1   This chapter is drawn, with permission from the publisher, from: "Israel and the Fencing Policy: A Barrier on Every Seam Line", research paper, Arab Center for Research and Policy Studies (June 2015), http://english.dohainstitute.org/file/get/847a306c-a229-44e4-9bc2-ad4ca6c4ffd6.pdf

2   See, for example, Uri Avnery's critical articles on Israeli separation walls.

3   Der Judenstaat (Leipzig and Vienna: M. Breitenstein's Verlags-Buchhandlung, 1896). English translation: *The Jewish State: An Attempt at a Modern Solution of the Jewish Question*, 6th ed. (New York: Maccabean Publishing Co., 1904). The title is also translated in English as *The State of the Jews*.

4   Theodor Herzl, *The Jewish State*, p. 28.

5   Uri Avnery, "First of All — the Wall must Fall", *Gush Shalom* (30 August 2003).

        https://doi.org/10.11647/OBP.0121.02

World"[6] and "The Ethics of the Iron Wall"[7] in which he defended the idea of establishing a metaphorical and, in many ways, physical "iron wall" between the populations, declaring that "Settlement can only develop under the protection of a force that is not dependent on the local population, behind an iron wall which they will be powerless to break down…"[8] At the time, Jabotinsky's "iron wall" doctrine was not adopted by the Zionist movement. Instead, it adopted the solution of expelling and displacing native Arab Palestinians.

Though each modern Israeli barrier has been built in its own specific context, the goals of each project of separation overlap and, in fact, form part of a policy of Israeli walls and fences derived from a single Zionist philosophy. This has translated into a state with perpetual security concerns, a lasting occupation, and the annexation of more Palestinian lands. Regardless of international resolutions recognizing the existence of the "Jewish state" within the so-called 1949 Armistice lines, the way and the context in which Israel was created and expanded has left it in an abnormal and hostile situation. Even if most Arab countries recognize, if implicitly, the State of Israel, their peoples have never accepted a normalization of relations with the "Jewish State" as an embodiment of principles that include a continuation of practices that are fundamentally separating "civilization" from its "others". Being at the center of the state's foundation and its current hostile predicament, the separation barrier policy can be said to reflect in many ways the constant fear in which Israel lives.

This chapter analyzes multiple aspects of Israel's policy of separation, and evaluates the effectiveness of its contemporary methods in order to determine whether or not such a policy makes Israel more secure. It begins by identifying three categories of barriers based on their geographical location: separation barriers in the occupied Palestinian territories (barriers separating Israelis from Palestinians and barriers

---

6   It was originally published in Russian in *Rassvyet* [Berlin] (4 November 1923), and later translated and published in English in *The Jewish Herald* [South Africa] (November 26, 1937).

7   Originally published in Russian in *Rassvyet* [Paris] (11 November 1923), and later translated and published in English in *The Jewish Standard* [London] (5 September 1941).

8   Ze'ev Jabotinsky, *The Iron Wall: Israel and the Arab World*, cited by Yosef Gorny, *Zionism and the Arabs: A Study of Ideology*, Translated by Chaya Galai (Oxford: Clarendon Press, 1987), p. 166.

separating Palestinians from each other), barriers as *de facto* borders between Israel and Arab countries and Israeli military barriers in other occupied Arab territories (e.g., in Egypt's Sinai Peninsula and the Syrian Golan Heights).

Separation Barriers in the Occupied Palestinian Territories: Dispersion of Population and Annexation of Territory

Israel has made the occupied Palestinian territories (oPt) a zone of separation barriers by surrounding itself by fortified walls and fences on every boundary line. Barriers that separate Palestinians from each other — mainly the West Bank wall — are the most painful not only because they are seen as major Israeli land-grabs but also because they affect vital aspects of Palestinian lives, especially for those who live in areas adjacent to the barriers.

The West Bank Separation Wall

In 1995, then-prime minister Yitzhak Rabin proposed building a separation wall[9] along the entire length of the West Bank including east Jerusalem, but the project was not pursued for fear of the reaction of Jewish settlers who saw the idea as a retreat from the project of absorbing the West Bank into a "Greater Israel". In March 1996, the Israeli government decided to establish checkpoints along the *de facto* borders of the West Bank, similar to the Erez checkpoint that controls the movement of people in and out of the Gaza Strip. In November 2000, the government of Ehud Barak approved a plan to establish a "barrier to prevent the passage of motor vehicles" from the northwest end of the West Bank to the Latrun area in the center. On 18 July 2001, the Israeli Ministerial Committee for Security Matters approved the recommendations of a steering committee established the previous month by then-Prime

---

9   Different terms are used to denote the Israeli separation wall in the West Bank. Israeli officials and journalists generally use two terms "separation fence" and "security fence" while Palestinians use mainly "apartheid wall" or "racial separation wall" (in Arabic, *jidar al-fasl al-unsuri*). The International Court of Justice, in its advisory opinion, used the term "separation wall", which I adopt in this chapter.

Minister Ariel Sharon, to adopt a series of measures aimed at preventing Palestinians from infiltrating into Israel across what became known as the "seam area". In April 2002, after a surge in attacks by Palestinian groups, the Israeli cabinet decided to construct a long barrier composed of fences and walls in three areas of the West Bank deemed to be the most vulnerable to penetration by armed Palestinians: the Umm El-Fahm region and the villages divided between Israel and the area (Baka and Barta'a), the Qalqilya-Tulkarm region and the Greater Jerusalem region. In June 2002, the Israeli government began building the separation wall. On 20 February 2005, after several amendments made over the previous three years, the Israeli government published a new map marking the Wall's route throughout the West Bank.[10]

The construction of the separation wall is linked by Samer Alatout to the third phase of Israel's occupation of the West Bank and Gaza which started in 1967. Alatout has shown how each period of occupation was guided by a distinct government own regime: the 1967–1994 period, marked by its initial occupation and subsequent establishment of intensive control over territory and population; the 1994–2002 period, when Israeli authorities adopted a new policy of cantonization through intensive use of roadblocks, checkpoints and bypass roads; and the current phase, which started in 2002, when the construction of the separation wall began.[11] These three phases, however, are not disconnected but rather overlap each other. For example, elements of the two earlier phases — such as occupation, control and cantonization — form an integral part of the latest phase of the Israeli separation policy.

---

10   This brief chronology of the construction of the West Bank wall is based on the Yehezkel Lein's article "Behind the Barrier: Human Rights Violations as a Result of Israel's Separation Barrier", position paper, Trans. Zvi Shulman, *B'Tselem* (March 2003),   https://www.btselem.org/download/200304_behind_the_barrier_eng.pdf. See also United Nations, "Humanitarian Impact of the West Bank Barrier", A report to the Humanitarian Emergency Policy Group (HEPG), compiled by the United Nations Office for Coordination of Humanitarian Affairs (OCHA) and the United Nations Relief and Works Agency for Palestine Refugees (UNRWA) in the occupied Palestinian territory, No. 6 (2006), https://unispal.un.org/DPA/DPR/unispal.nsf/0/1 FE4606B31BC49748525713900575924

11   Samer Alatout, "Walls as Technologies of Government: The Double Construction of Geographies of Peace and Conflict in Israeli Politics, 2002-Present", *Annals of the Association of American Geographers*, Vol. 99, No. 5 (2009), p. 960, http://dces. wisc.edu/wp-content/uploads/sites/30/2013/08/The-Israeli-Separation-Wall-and-Technologies-of-Government-the-Double-Construction-of-Geographies-of-Peace-and-Conflict.pdf

While the construction of the separation wall in the West Bank obviously reflected a new phase of the Israeli policy towards the oPt, it, in addition to the annexation of some parts of West Bank territory to Israel, this new policy resulted in a unilateral separation of Israel from other Palestinian occupied lands.

Map and Structure of the West Bank Separation Wall

Close to 90 percent of the total route of the wall is inside the West Bank,[12] chewing up the land to the East of the Green Line — the pre-1967 border between Israel and what was then a Jordanian-administered West Bank. Effectively, the separation wall does not only separate Palestinians from Israel but separates Palestinians from their land, hence Palestinians' contention that one of the major goals in erecting the West Bank wall is to annex more Palestinian lands to nearby Israeli settlements, and, thus, to Israel. The total length of the separation wall extends approximately 750 kilometers, more than twice the length of the 320 kilometer-long Green Line (1949 Armistice Line),[13] since it zigzags into the West Bank up to 22 kilometers at points to ensure settlements fall on its western edge. The wall has an average width of 60–80 meters, which includes a system of barbed wire, ditches, large trace paths and tank-patrol lanes on each side, as well as additional buffer zones/no-go areas of varying depths.[14]

The separation wall is a fully integrated military system of walls, fences (including electronic and barbed-wire fences), barriers, trenches, sensors, watchtowers, sandy routes, concrete slabs up to 8 metres high, thermal imaging, video cameras, aerial drones and other security measures. Amos Yaron, former director of Israel's Ministry of Defense, described the West Bank separation wall as "the largest project ever

---

12 Amnesty International, "Israel and the Occupied Territories: The Place of the Fence/Wall in International Law", https://www.amnesty.org/en/documents/MDE15/016/2004/en/

13 The 1949 Armistice lines (known also as the Green Line) refer to the demarcation lines between Israeli forces and those of neighboring Arab Countries, Egypt, Lebanon, Jordan, and Syria, which defined by the agreements that put an end to the 1984 Arab-Israeli War. These lines served as the *de facto* border of Israel until the 1967 war.

14 *Ibid.*

undertaken in Israel".[15] Although the structure of the separation wall takes various physical forms, it can be summarized in the following points:

- Barbed wire, to obstruct access.

- A trench 4 meters wide and 5 meters deep, dug behind the barbed wires.

- A paved road 12 meters wide, which is a military road for surveillance and reconnaissance.

- A sand road 4 meters wide located right behind the military road, to trace infiltrators. This road is combed twice daily, in the morning and evening.

- The separation wall is situated right on the sand road. It is a 1-meter cement wall and right directly over it there is a 3-meter electronic fence, where alarms, surveillance cameras, lights, and other security apparatus are placed.

- After the wall, there is a sand road, a paved road, a trench, and barbed wire, mirroring the ones located on the other side of the wall.[16]

The construction of the separation wall in the West Bank is estimated to cost somewhere between NIS 10 million (USD 2.8 million) to NIS 15 million (USD 4.3 million) per kilometer.[17] Extra costs and those associated with 24-hour human and electronic surveillance put the total cost of the 750-kilometer Israeli separation wall somewhere between USD 2.1 and USD 3.2 billion.

The land area in the West Bank located between the separation wall and the Green Line has been designated by the Israeli government as

---

15   Felix Frisch, "Israel Plans: Tax to Be Imposed on Palestinians Who Enter Israel", *Y-net News* (6 March 2003).

16   The information on the barrier's structure is extracted from a report published by the Palestinian National Authority, The State Information Center, "The Israeli Racist Separation Wall: Consequences and Violations" (10 October 2003), http://w3.osaarchivum.org/galeria/the_divide/cpt14files/the_israeli_racist_separation_wall.doc. This information is consistent with what is reported in the Response of the Israeli State Attorney to the High Court of Justice in HCJ 7784/02, Sa' al 'Awani 'Abd al Hadi *et al.* v. Commander of IDF Forces in the West Bank, sec. 23.

17   Amos Harel, "Cost of Fence could Rise to NIS 15 Million per Kilometer", *Haaretz* (8 April 2004); Felix Frisch, "Israel Plans: Tax to Be Imposed on Palestinians Who Enter Israel".

a "seam zone" and declared a "closed zone". According to the Israeli military Declaration of Closing an Area No. S/20/03 made on 2 October 2003, "no person will enter the seam area and no one will remain there". This order, however, does not apply to Israelis or those who have the right to immigrate to Israel according to the country's Law of Return.[18] The Palestinians who live near the area are allowed to remain in their homes and on their lands only if they possess a written permit authorizing permanent residence. It is expected that, when the separation wall is finished as planned, approximately 65,000 Palestinians will require permits to cross the wall into the West Bank where they legally reside, and some 270,000 Palestinians living in these areas will be trapped in closed military areas between the wall and the Green Line or in enclaves encircled by the wall.[19] That these confiscated lands in the "seam area" include the West Bank's most valuable agricultural land and water resources measuring 73,000 dunums, a vital source of income for the Palestinians in the region, is another cause of concern for a failing Palestinian economy.

Fig. 1.1 The West Bank separation wall (17 August 2004).
Photo by Justin McIntosh, CC BY 2.0.[20]

---

18 Article 4, Israeli Law of Return.
19 *Ibid.*
20 Source: Wikimedia Commons, https://commons.wikimedia.org/wiki/File%3A Israeli_West_Bank_Barrier.jpg

Goals of the West Bank Separation Wall

The sole stated purpose of the separation wall, as repeatedly declared by the Israeli government, is a temporary structure providing security[21] by preventing, or at least reducing, attacks carried out by Palestinian militant groups against Israelis inside the Green Line. The decision to build the wall was taken after the outbreak of the Second Palestinian Uprising (Al-Aqsa Intifada) on 29 September 2000, when the former Likud leader Ariel Sharon, accompanied by thousands of Israeli security forces, visited the Haram Ash-Sharif, known to Jews as the Temple Mount, in al-Quds (Jerusalem). The Palestinians saw Sharon's visit as a provocation, and a new uprising quickly spread throughout the West Bank and Gaza Strip. From this point, the Arab-Israeli conflict entered a new phase, characterized by the escalation of bombing attacks inside Israel. In 2001 and 2002, Palestinian armed groups[22] carried out 87 bombings against Israeli targets, causing 299 fatalities.[23]

Palestinians reject Israel's justification of the construction of the wall based on a security argument and maintain that the wall was built for political reasons: to protect and perpetuate Israel's occupation, illegal colonies and ongoing colonization of the Palestinian land. Even if the decision to build the separation wall in 2000 was made in the context of a wave of attacks inside Israel, large numbers of the Palestinian attackers who carried out these operations passed through Israeli military checkpoints not through the porous border between Israel and the oPt.[24] The Palestine Liberation Organization (PLO) argues that if Israel truly wanted to protect its citizens, it should "do one or both of the following: withdraw completely from all of the territories it occupied

---

21 See, for example, the Israeli Government decision of 23 July 2001 cited in the website of Israel Seam Zone Authority.

22 These attacks were carried out in particular by those affiliated with Hamas, Palestinian Islamic Jihad (PIJ), Fatah, and Popular Front for the Liberation of Palestine (PFLP).

23 Efraim Benmelech and Claude Berrebi, "Human Capital and the Productivity of Suicide Bombers", *Journal of Economic Perspectives*, Vol. 21, No. 3 (2007), p. 226.

24 Palestinian Centre for Human Rights, "Securing the Wall from International Law: An Initial Response to the Israeli State Attorney", position paper, Palestinian Centre for Human Rights (2005).

in 1967 or place additional security on its internationally-recognized border, rather than in the occupied Palestinian territories".[25]

In addition to the wall that annexed between 10 to 15 percent of the West Bank, the Israeli settlements, in this part of the oPt, are also a land grab and contravene international law.[26] As of 2004, some 54 Israeli settlements in the West Bank and 12 in East Jerusalem were located on Palestinian land that is being cut off from the rest of the West Bank by the wall and being *de facto* annexed to Israel. In total, more than 320,000 Israeli settlers, some 80 percent of the settlers living in the oPt, will be living on the western side of the wall and will thus enjoy more direct territorial contiguity with Israel.[27] In contrast, around 67 Palestinian villages are separated from Palestinian communities, including their means of livelihood and access to government services. Some 210,000 are barred in isolated enclaves, in severe violation of their rights under international law.[28] Through the construction of its separation wall, then, Israel is drawing a new *de facto* map and unilaterally redefining its borders.

Some argue that if it was only about a temporary security measure, Israel could construct a barbed-wire fence that would perform the same function and could easily be dismantled or destroyed, instead of a steel-reinforced concrete wall. Indeed, its cost and route both seem to disprove claims that it is a temporary structure.

Effects of the West Bank Separation Wall

The Social Impact

According to international law, Israel, as an occupying power, is obliged to respect the fundamental rights of the occupied Palestinian population at all times and to administer the Palestinian territory without making changes which could have far-reaching effects on the population or

---

25 PLO Negotiations Affairs Department, "Bad Fences Make Bad Neighbors", *The Palestine-Israel Journal*, Vol. 9, No. 3 (2002).

26 Amnesty International, "Israel and the Occupied Territories: The issue of Settlements must be Addressed according to International Law" (8 September 2003).

27 Amnesty International, "Israel and the Occupied Territories", p. 4.

28 Yehezkel Lein, "Behind the Barrier: Human Rights Violations As a Result of Israel's Separation Barrier", position paper, Trans. Zvi Shulman, *B'Tselem* (April 2003), pp. 4–9.

territory. The separation wall undoubtedly has a high human cost, one that is increasing still further the suffering of the Palestinian people. Since the construction of the wall began in 2002, human rights organizations have documented the immediate human impact of the wall. Reported effects, which present serious violations of both international human rights and international humanitarian law, affect various aspects of the Palestinians' economic and social activities, including restrictions on movement, as well as the destruction and seizure of land. Amnesty International, for example, has repeatedly asserted that the wall cannot be considered a necessary or proportionate security measure and does not benefit the local Palestinian population. On the contrary, it is regarded as an act of collective punishment, which is forbidden by international humanitarian law (Article 33 of the Fourth Geneva Convention, and the restrictions allowed by Article 64 of the same Convention). Moreover, the wall has severely negative consequences for hundreds of thousands of Palestinians, including unprecedented, disproportionate and discriminatory restrictions on their movements within the oPt, as well as other violations of their fundamental rights, including the right to work, to food, to medical care, to education and to an adequate standard of living.[29]

Thousands of Palestinians living inside the Green Line and near the separation wall find themselves separated not only from their agricultural lands but also from their nearby communities.

A report issued by the UN Office for the Coordination of Humanitarian Affairs (OCHA) in June 2007 summarized the significant humanitarian and social effects of the separation wall on Palestinian life in the following findings:

- Palestinians from the West Bank require permits to visit the six specialist hospitals inside Jerusalem. The resulting time and difficulty this entails has meant an up to 50% drop in the number of patients visiting these hospitals.

- Entire families have been divided by the wall. Husbands and wives are separated from each other, their children and other relatives.

---

29   Amnesty International, "Israel and the Occupied Territories: The Place of the Fence/ Wall in International Law" (19 February 2004), p. 6

- Palestinian Muslims and Christians can no longer freely visit religious sites in Jerusalem. Permits are needed and are increasingly difficult to obtain.

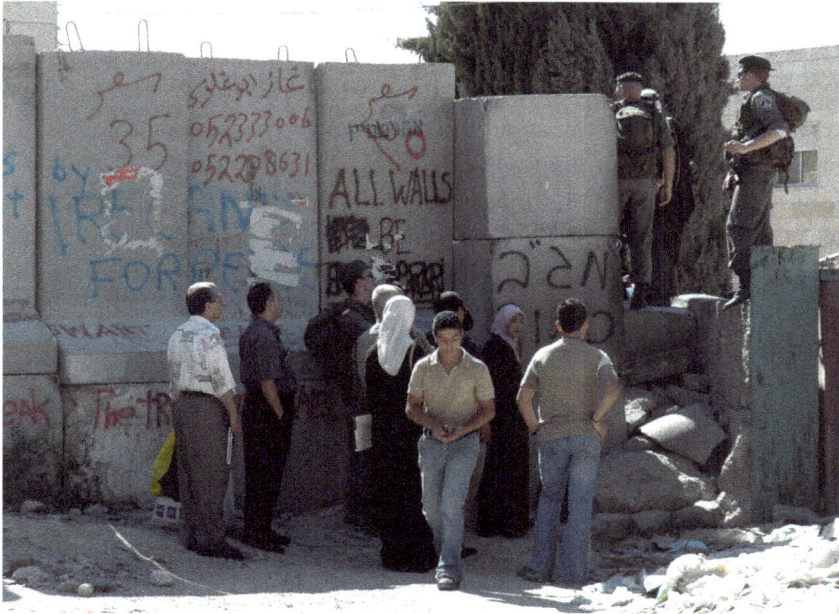

Fig. 1.2 A checkpoint in the West Bank Separation Wall, near Abu Dis (18 August 2004). Photo by Justin McIntosh, CC BY 2.0.[30]

School and university students struggle each day through checkpoints to reach institutions that are located on the other side of the wall. Entire communities, such as the 15,000 people in the villages of the Bir Nabala enclave, are totally surrounded by the wall. The only way in or out is through a tunnel to Ramallah which passes under the motorway that is restricted for Israeli use only.[31]

---

30 Source: Wikimedia Commons, https://commons.wikimedia.org/wiki/File%3A Checkpoint_near_Abu_Dis.jpg

31 Office for the Coordination of Humanitarian Affairs (OCHA) United Nations Relief and Works Agency for Palestine Refugees in the Near East (UNRWA), "Humanitarian Impact of the West Bank Barrier on Palestinian Communities", Report No. 7 (June 2007), p. 4, https://unispal.un.org/DPA/DPR/unispal.nsf/0/1FE4 606B31BC49748525713900575924

The Economic Effects

When construction of the wall began, studies by humanitarian organizations expected its immediate economic effects to include "a) the destruction of agricultural land and assets and water resources; b) inaccessibility to agricultural land and assets; c) added limitations on the mobility of people and goods, and therefore higher transactions costs; and d) uncertainty about the future and a consequent dampening of investment in economic activities including agriculture".[32] This was indeed the case. The Palestinian governorates adjacent to the separation wall; especially in Jenin, Tulkarm and Qalqiliya; are the most directly affected by its construction. The economic impact of the wall on these regions recorded immediately after its construction has been substantial, due principally to restrictions on farming and the inaccessibility of land by its owners. These areas, once known as the breadbasket of Palestine, are home to 37 percent of all the agricultural land in the West Bank.

Movement restrictions have proved fatal for many whose livelihoods are made in agriculture, and increased unemployment rates are seen in areas close to the wall.[33] Furthermore, it is very difficult for many Palestinians to obtain a permit to enter the seam area. Even if some Palestinian farmers can get a permit to enter, they are not guaranteed regular access to their land for several reasons, including:

- Restrictions on the period of time a farmer can be in the closed areas.

- The Israeli army's control of the gates is so erratic that this is as much a problem as the permit regime itself.

- Agricultural gates are open three times a day, generally for 20 minutes to an hour.

- Following a security incident, the gates can be closed for several days or more.

---

32 The Humanitarian and Emergency Policy Group (HEPG) and the Local Aid Coordination Committee (LACC), "The Impact of Israel's Separation Barrier on Affected West Bank Communities" (4 May 2003), p. 11.

33 United Nations, "Humanitarian Impact of the West Bank Barrier", No. 6, p. 8, https:// unispal.un.org/DPA/DPR/unispal.nsf/0/1FE4606B31BC49748525713900575924

- Tractors and other farm vehicles are frequently not permitted to cross the gate. Farmers must either walk or use a donkey to reach their land and bring out produce.

- Each permit is valid for a particular gate. Some farmers have the wrong gate numbers on their permits, leaving access for the farmer reliant on a soldier's discretion.[34]

In addition to the effects of the wall on agricultural activity, cutting off Palestinian communities from their primary income streams both within the West Bank and Israel has deepened the isolation of the regions adjacent to the wall. For, while the wall separates Palestinians from their farmland and water sources and impedes their movement of produce to market in other areas of the West Bank, it also makes it difficult for tens of thousands of Palestinians to access work in Israel, mainly as day laborers on farms or construction sites, a primary source of income for many. The danger is that serious economic and social effects of the wall will likely push some Palestinians to move, a form of indirect forced displacement and ethnic cleansing.

It is worth mentioning that the construction of the wall does not only affect Palestinians living in the oPt but also thousands of Palestinians living in the Green Line near the separation wall. They also find themselves cut off from their agricultural lands and their nearby compatriots both in the West Bank and across the Green Line.

The Environmental Cost

Vital environmental resources in the "seam area/buffer zone" of the separation wall are destroyed by the wall. The effects of the confiscation of water wells, the demolition of homes and greenhouses and the uprooting of hundreds of thousands of trees and crops are devastating. Palestinians argue that Israel, through the wall and its associated regime, will dominate all the strategic sites of fresh water in the region, especially in Jenin, Qalqilya and Tulkarm. The Palestinian Authority has accused Israel of planning to gain control over the most important Palestinian

---

34   *Ibid.*, p. 9.

water resources when it set out the route of the wall.[35] Palestinians therefore fear that the situation will further weaken the Palestinian position in any future negotiations over water.[36]

The Effect on Jerusalem

Jerusalem, which remains the thorniest issue when it comes to the resolution of the Arab-Israeli conflict, will be deeply affected by the construction of the separation wall by isolating the Holy City from its environs and the West Bank. The largest part of East Jerusalem will be swallowed and absorbed by the separation wall into Israel.[37] Palestinians assert that one of the hidden goals of separating east Jerusalem from the West Bank is to control the movement of Palestinians to and from the city, thereby forcing Palestinians living there to move eastwards and out of the Palestinian capital. This would cause a dramatic change in the demographic balance of Jerusalem in favor of its Jewish population. This is part of a documented program of Judaizing the city that began in the 1970s, according to a number of studies. They assert that Israel has worked to uproot Palestinians in the Holy City and to separate Jerusalem from its geographical and historical connections.

The International Legal Status of the West Bank Separation Wall

On 8 December 2003, the UN General Assembly requested an advisory opinion from the International Court of Justice (ICJ) on the legal consequences of the construction of the Israeli separation wall, considering the rules and principles of international law, including the fourth Geneva Convention of 1949, and relevant Security Council and General Assembly resolutions. On 9 July 2004, the ICJ issued its advisory

---

35   Palestinian National Authority and PWA, The Israeli Apartheid Separation Wall "To Control The Palestinian Water Resources", prepared by the PWA in cooperation with Sustainable Management of the West Bank and Gaza Aquifer (5 February 2003), p. 2.

36   Palestinian National Authority, State Information Center, "The Israeli Racist Separation Wall", http://w3.osaarchivum.org/galeria/the_divide/cpt14files/the_israeli_racist_separation_wall.doc

37   Peter Lagerquist, "Fencing the Last Sky: Excavating Palestine after Israel's 'Separation Wall'", *Journal of Palestine Studies*, Vol. 33, No. 2 (2004), p. 15.

opinion on the matter, stating that the construction of the wall and its associated regime could well become permanent, notwithstanding the formal characterization of the wall by Israel, in which case it would be tantamount to a *de facto* annexation (para. 121).[38]

The court rejected Israel's security argument since the route of the wall and its associated regime gravely infringe a number of rights of Palestinians residing in the territory occupied by Israel, and the infringements resulting from that route cannot be justified by military need or by the requirements of national security or public order (para. 137). The court also called on Israel to comply with its obligation to respect the right of the Palestinian people to self-determination and its obligations under international humanitarian law and international human rights law (para. 149). The advisory opinion of the ICJ included five main findings (para. 163):

1. The construction of the wall is contrary to international law.

2. Israel is under an obligation to terminate its breaches of international law; to cease forthwith the works of construction of the wall, to dismantle forthwith the structure therein situated, and to repeal or render ineffective forthwith all legislative and regulatory acts relating thereto.

3. Israel is under an obligation to make reparation for all damage caused by the construction of the wall.

4. All States are under an obligation not to recognize the illegal situation resulting from the construction of the wall and not to render aid or assistance in maintaining the situation created by such construction; all States parties to the Fourth Geneva Convention relative to the Protection of Civilian Persons in Time of War of 12 August 1949, have, in addition the obligation, while respecting the United Nations Charter and international law, to ensure compliance by Israel with international humanitarian law as embodied in that Convention.

---

38 Advisory Opinion Concerning Legal Consequences of the Construction of a Wall in the Occupied Palestinian Territory, International Court of Justice (ICJ), 9 July 2004, http://www.refworld.org/cases,ICJ,414ad9a719.html

5. The United Nations should consider what further action is required to bring to an end the illegal situation resulting from the construction of the wall and the associated regime.

These findings were adopted almost unanimously by the fifteen participating judges of the ICJ. Two exceptions were Judge Buergenthal, who voted against the five findings, and Judge Kooijmans, who voted for the advisory opinion except the fourth finding. Given the complexity of the case and the huge levels of Israeli lobbying that came ahead of the decision, this remarkable consensus on the legal consequences of the separation wall gives these findings a significant and enduring place in the jurisprudence of the ICJ.[39]

Gaza Fences

Gaza has been under Israeli military occupation since the Six-Day War in 1967, even though UN Resolution 242, passed on 22 November 1967 in the aftermath of the war, called for Israel to withdraw "from territories occupied in the recent conflict", including Gaza. Israel declared the Gaza Strip a closed military zone — a declaration that was in place until 2005 — which meant that Palestinians in Gaza had to obtain permission from Israel whenever they wanted to travel out of the closed zone. Despite Israel's unilateral withdrawal from Gaza in 2005 and the transfer of the management of the Gaza-Egypt border crossing at Rafah to the European Union Border Assistance Mission (EUBAM), Israel continued to exercise remote control of the crossing via closed-circuit cameras until 2007. This followed Hamas' landslide victory in the Palestinian parliamentary election of 2006 and the subsequent struggle for control between Hamas and Fatah, which saw Hamas take over the Gaza Strip in 2007. Israel's blockade of the Gaza Strip was part of the state's reaction to a loss of control of the enclave, but the blockade has only been possible with the acquiescence of Egypt and its leaders.

---

39 Richard A. Falk, "Toward Authoritativeness: The ICJ Ruling on Israel's Security Wall", *The American Journal of International Law*, Vol. 99, No. 1 (2005), p. 43

In October 1994, after a string of attacks carried by Palestinian militant groups in the coastal city of Tel Aviv, Israeli Prime Minister Yitzhak Rabin called for the construction of a fence around the Gaza Strip. The aim was both to separate Israelis from Palestinians and to cut off Gaza's Palestinian residents from the rest of the world. Rabin based his proposal on a philosophy of separation rooted in Zionist thought by stating, "We have to decide on separation as a philosophy. There has to be a clear border. Without a border demarcating the lines, whoever wants to swallow 1.8 million Arabs will just bring greater support for Hamas".[40] Israel has built two metal barriers around the Gaza Strip, one between Israel and Gaza and the other along the border of Gaza with Egypt. The structure, constructed in 1994–1996, is 51 kilometers long and made mostly of barbed wire and corrugated sheet metal. At the beginning of 2000, al-Aqsa Intifada, Palestinian activists dismantled much of the barrier, which was rebuilt by the Israeli military between December 2000 and June 2001, with the addition of observation posts, each of which enabled soldiers to monitor an area of roughly 6 kilometers round-the-clock.[41] When Israel found that the direct military occupation of the Gaza Strip was more costly than anticipated, it decided to withdraw from the Strip and maintain complete control from outside its borders, ultimately turning Gaza into an extended prison.

On the other side, and further separating Gaza from its environs, a fence was constructed along Gaza's land border with Egypt in 2004–2005 by Israel. This came in parallel with the "unilateral withdrawal" of settlers from Gaza and the end of internal Israeli control. Israel still exercises almost complete control over Gaza's land borders, territorial waters and airspace and prevents significant contact between the population there and the outside world. The Israeli fence between Gaza and Egypt is 11 kilometers (6.8 miles) long and 7–9 meters (about 20–30 feet) high, with several openings that allow the Israeli army to move through it under special circumstances. Because Palestinians built underground tunnels in order to smuggle items such as food

---

40   David Makovsky, "How to Build a Fence", *Foreign Affairs*, Vol. 83, No. 2 (2004), p. 52.

41   Doron Almog, "Lessons of the Gaza Security Fence for the West Bank", *Jerusalem Issue Brief*, Jerusalem Center for Public Affairs, Vol. 4, No. 12 (2004).

and weapons from Egypt, the Israeli army equipped the fence with sophisticated technology and sensors that can detect such tunnels and aid in their destruction.[42] Tunnels in Rafah on the Gaza-Egypt border manage to evade total Israeli control, despite the army's attempts to destroy them by aerial bombardment.

The Israeli fence along Gaza's perimeter has three main crossings through which Palestinians and their goods can enter and leave the territory: Beit Hanoun (Erez) in the north, for those going to and from Israel, imposes stringent restrictions on the movement of Palestinians; al-Montar (Karni) crossing to the east, which handles cargo and has been closed since the beginning of the al-Aqsa Intifada; and the Rafah crossing to the south, on the Egyptian border, which was monitored by the Israel Airports Authority until Israel withdrew from Gaza on 11 September 2005 as part of Israel's unilateral disengagement plan. It was subsequently managed by the EUBAM until Hamas took over the Gaza Strip in 2007.

Evidence of the ineffectiveness of the separation fences to stop attacks emanating from Gaza can perhaps best be seen in the constant wars waged by Israel on the Strip. Despite the separation fences, regular military invasions, aerial bombings, targeted assassinations and land confiscations continue to be carried out.[43] From 2006, three large-scale attacks have been waged on Gaza, the second of which, in December 2008-January 2009, killed approximately 1,417 Palestinians. The construction of the fence along the perimeter of the Gaza Strip has also not stopped attacks by Palestinian militant groups, since the organizations have adopted new means to fight Israel that include the use of surface-to-surface missiles and rockets that can reach Israeli cities on the other side of the barrier.

The barrier has failed to ensure Israeli security, has undermined Palestinian territorial integrity and caused harm to the civilian population there.

---

42 Hanan Greenberg, "Army Building New Gaza Barrier", *Y-net News* (4 April 2005), http://www.ynetnews.com/articles/0,7340,L-3072620,00.html

43 Palestinian Centre for Human Rights, "Securing the Wall from International Law: An Initial Response to the Israeli State Attorney", position paper (April 2005).

De Facto Borders: Similar Purposes in Different Contexts

Lebanon-Israel Border Fences

During the British Mandate for Palestine, double and triple barbed-wire fences along the Palestine-Lebanon border were constructed between May and June 1938 in an attempt to seal off the border against incursions from the north of Palestine. The barrier was dismantled during the 1936–1939 Arab uprisings in Palestine. At the same time, the British Mandatory authorities erected a new barbed wire called Tergart's Wall on the northern border of Palestine to prevent Arab militants from Syria and Lebanon from joining the 1936–1939 revolt. Tergart's Wall was abandoned and dismantled during World War II.

With the end of the British Mandate (after the establishment of the State of Israel), the Israeli government built new fences running the length of the Palestine-Lebanon border. In 1976, the government adopted a security policy toward southern Lebanon called "the Good Fence", aimed at providing some services to southern Lebanese people, especially the Maronites, including passage into Israel for work, access to medical treatment, Israeli goods, relief support, water and food supplies[44] and even military assistance and training for "those seeking to defend their community".[45] This policy was intended to support the South Lebanon Army (Maronite Militia) in its battle against the PLO during the Lebanese civil war which broke out in 1976. The "Good Fence" policy ceased to exist with the sudden withdrawal of Israeli troops from southern Lebanon in 2000.

In the 1970s, Israel built a fence without respecting the exact lines of the border inherited from the Mandate period.[46] After the 1983–1984 withdrawal of Israeli troops from most of Lebanon except for the "security zone" in the south, Israel built a sophisticated defense complex along the border, consisting of electrified fences, anti-personnel

---

44 Augustus Richard Norton and Jillian Schwedler, "(In) security Zones in South Lebanon", *Journal of Palestine Studies*, Vol. 23, No. 1 (1993), p. 63.

45 Clive H. Schofield, "Elusive Security: The Military and Political Geography of South Lebanon", *GeoJournal*, Vol. 31, No. 2 (1993), p. 155.

46 Joseph Algazy, "Soiled Hands, spoiled Lands", *Haaretz* (24 December 1999) cited in Julie Trottier, "A Wall, Water and Power: the Israeli 'Separation Fence'", *Review of International Studies*, Vol. 33, No. 1 (2007), p. 108.

minefields, patrol roads and barbed-wire obstacles.[47] In March 1985, after a truck bombing in southern Lebanon killed 12 Israeli soldiers, Israel extended and moved the border fence to the northwest. The modern fence on the Israel-Lebanon border is considered the backbone of Israel's passive defense on its northern border. The fence consists of barbed wire; movement sensors and infra-red, radio, television and electronic monitors at strategic points that can locate any intrusion within 500 meters; routine road patrols along the security road and fine sand that allows the detection of footprints.[48] Though equipped with the latest technology ostensibly making infiltration nearly impossible, the fence failed to prevent Hezbollah fighters from penetrating into Israel on 12 July 2006. They killed five soldiers and took two of the bodies back north into Lebanon. The event led to the outbreak of a 34-day war between Israel and Hezbollah. Even during periods of relative calm, the *de facto* Israeli-Lebanon border remains a battlefield.

Egypt's Underground Wall

In early December 2009, Egypt started, under the pretext of national security, to construct an underground steel wall that extended down 35 meters (115ft) for approximately 12 kilometers along its border with the Gaza Strip. The stated aim of the wall was to block Palestinian tunnels, which have been in operation since at least 1982. The tunnels were built during that year's peace treaty by Palestinian families who had been divided between Israeli-occupied Gaza and Egyptian-controlled Rafah. The underground tunnels linked Gaza and Egypt as a means of communication amongst extended family members.[49]

The underground obstruction to these tunnels is made of steel sheets and sensors and is connected to pipes that can collapse tunnels dug

47   David Eshel, "The Israel-Lebanon Border Enigma", *IBRU Boundary and Security Bulletin*, Vol. 8, No. 4 (2000–2001), p. 80.

48   See, for example, Al J. Venter, "Israel Last Line of Defense", *Jane's International Defense Review*, Vol. 29 No. 11 (1996), p. 61; David Eshel, "Counter-guerrilla Warfare in South Lebanon", *Marine Corps Gazette*, No. 1 (1997), p. 42; Julie Trottier, "A Wall, Water and Power: The Israeli 'Separation Fence'", *Review of International Studies*, p. 108.

49   Jeremy Sharp, "The Egypt-Gaza Border and its Effect on Israeli-Egyptian Relations", Congressional Research Service, Report No. RL34346 (1 February 2008), http://www.fas.org/sgp/crs/mideast/RL34346.pdf

into the sandy earth by saturating the ground along the border with pumped-in seawater.[50] NGOs warned of an environmental disaster if the seawater pumped under the barrier leaked into the only underground freshwater wells available to the local population for drinking and agriculture purposes. The wall makes tunnel digging even more dangerous than it already was.

It has been widely reported that the underground wall was built in response to U.S. and Israeli pressure to close the tunnels, including Washington's threat to cut military aid to Egypt over concern about arms smuggling through these passageways. The Consolidated Appropriations Act of 2008, signed into law on 26 December 2007, would have withheld USD 100 million in Foreign Military Financing from Egypt until then the U.S. Secretary of State, Condoleezza Rice, reported that Cairo had taken concrete steps to detect and destroy the smuggling tunnels leading from Egypt to Gaza.[51] The U.S. military designed the wall and gave significant technical and financial assistance to the Egyptian government for its construction. In 2008, as a response to pressure from the U.S., Egypt agreed to spend USD 23 million in U.S. military aid on robots and other advanced technology to detect smuggling tunnels and accepted an American offer to send experts from the Army Corps of Engineers to train Egyptian border guards in the technology.[52]

However, smuggling across the Egypt-Gaza border does not pose a threat to Egyptian national security. Rather, it alleviates the suffering of the Palestinian population caused by the Israeli-imposed blockade. Egypt's underground wall does not protect Egypt; rather it enables Cairo to protect its own interests, which means protecting the interests of the United States and, through them, of Israel. The wall strangles the only lifeline available to the Palestinians in Gaza. This has resulted in a humanitarian disaster.

---

50 Ursula Lindsey, "Egypt's Wall", *Middle East Research and Information Project* (1 February 2010), http://www.merip.org/mero/mero020110

51 Carol Migdalovitz, "Israel: Background and Relations with the United States", Congressional Research Service (2 April 2009), p. 19; Tally Helfont, "Egypt's Wall with Gaza & the Emergence of a New Middle East Alignment", *ORBIS*, Vol. 54, No. 3 (2010), p. 434.

52 Ellen Knickmeyer, "Egypt to Bolster Gaza Border" *Washington Post* (7 January 2008), http://www.washingtonpost.com/wp-dyn/content/article/2008/01/06/AR2008 010602055.html

Many human rights organizations have strongly condemned the construction of the underground wall, labeling it a collective punishment and therefore an offense under international humanitarian law. The UK-based Arab Organization for Human Rights (AOHR) considers the barrier's presence to be a crime against humanity, noting that the wall aims to tighten the noose around the people of Gaza, to break their will and impose agendas which are hostile to the Palestinians' rights to freedom and self-determination.[53] Although any state has the right to build and to protect its national security, international law restricts this right to avoid damage to neighboring countries. Therefore, Egypt, because of its status as the only gateway on the other side of Gaza, is required under international law to cease the construction of the barrier and to dismantle what is already built, as well as to open the Rafah crossing to save the Gaza population from what amounts to an Israeli blockade.

Sinai Fence

In 2010, following the smuggling of tens of thousands of African migrants mainly from Sudan, Ethiopia and Eritrea across the Sinai Peninsula and into Israel, the Israeli government prepared plans for the construction of a border fence along its Sinai border with Egypt. The aim was to prevent the entry of African "infiltrators" (the stigmatizing term used by Israelis) and arms smugglers into Israeli territory. Such a fence would "secure Israel's Jewish and democratic character" because it would stunt the growth of the non-Jewish population that could undermine its "Jewish character" and its Zionist dream.

The Israeli Ministry of Defense initially declared that by the end of 2011 the fence would cover the 240 kilometer-long porous border with Egypt.[54] The main section of the fence was completed in early 2013,[55]

---

53   Arab Organization for Human Rights in the UK (AOHR), "Special Report. Egyptian Government Infected by Mad Israeli Wall Disease" (30 December 2009), https://www.middleeastmonitor.com/wp-content/uploads/downloads/other_reports/the-arab-organisation-of-human-rights-in-the-uk-egypt-wall.pdf

54   Ben Hartman, "First Permanent Section of Sinai Border Fence Completed", *The Jerusalem Post* (2 June 2011), http://www.jpost.com/Defense/First-permanent-section-of-Sinai-border-fence-completed

55   Joshua Mitnick, "Israel Finishes Most of Fence on Sinai Border", *The Wall Street Journal* (2 January 2013), http://online.wsj.com/article/SB10001424127887324374004578217720772159626.html

and, once fully complete, the entire fence is expected to have cost about NIS 1.5 billion (USD 395 million).[56] It is constructed of barbed wire and will include high-tech surveillance cameras and radar equipment that will alert the military to intruders.

Even if infiltration of the border by African migrants has dropped significantly since the construction of the fence began in November 2010, as Israeli officials have stated,[57] the system will likely increase the number of those migrants who die trying to cross into Israel through more remote desert areas in the Sinai Peninsula.

Jordan-Israel Border Fence

Until 1994, Jordan's recognized border with Israel was based on the armistice line[58] agreed to in April 1949 by Israel and what was then Transjordan, following negotiations facilitated by the UN.[59] Today, the international boundary between Israel and Jordan is delimited by the Peace Treaty signed between the two sides in 1994, based on principles contained in UN Security Council resolutions 242 of 1967 and 338 of 1973, making Jordan the second Arab country after Egypt to normalize relations with Israel. The Treaty delineated the international border between Israel and Jordan with reference to the boundary defined under the British Mandate (Article 3).

Although the Israeli-Jordan border remains the least turbulent of Israel's frontiers, it is marked by a barbed-wire fence separating the two

---

56 Barak Ravid, "Israel to Build NIS 1.5b Fence Along Egypt Border", *Haaretz* (1 October 2010), http://www.haaretz.com/israel-to-build-nis-1-5b-fence-along-egypt-border-1.261141

57 See for example: Harriet Sherwood, "Israeli border fence halts migrant flood from Egypt", *The Sydney Morning Herald*, 2 January 2013, http://www.smh.com.au/world/israeli-border-fence-halts-migrant-flood-from-egypt-20130101-2c44j.html#ixzz2PY00GLtx; Harriet Sherwood, "Israeli fence construction cuts off migration from Egypt", *The Guardian*, 31 December 2012, https://www.theguardian.com/world/2012/dec/31/israeli-fence-cuts-migration-egypt; Miriam Valverde, "Border fence in Israel cut illegal immigration by 99 percent", 13 February 2017, *Politifact*, http://www.politifact.com/truth-o-meter/statements/2017/feb/13/ron-johnson/border-fence-israel-cut-illegal-immigration-99-per/

58 The 1949 Armistice Agreements are a set of agreements signed in the year 1949 between Israel and its immediate neighbors, Egypt, Lebanon, Jordan and Syria.

59 Colonel Mazen Qojas, "Cooperative Border Security for Jordan: Assessment and Options", *Cooperative Monitoring Center Occasional Papers/8* (March 1999), p. 20, http://www.sandia.gov/cooperative-monitoring-center/_assets/documents/sand98-05058.pdf

countries from the Dead Sea to the Red Sea. Israel has not fenced its entire 238-kilometer boundary with Jordan, however, since the segment along the shore of the Dead Sea is not fenced. Much of the remaining border, though, is lined by a patrol road with fences on either side.[60] Some segments of the fence were taken down following the 1994 treaty.

In March 2011, Israeli Prime Minister Benjamin Netanyahu said he had instructed the military to begin planning the construction of a new fence along the border with Jordan. Israel gives great importance to the project because, according to Netanyahu, once the fence with Egypt is erected, smugglers and infiltrators will look for alternative routes to enter Israel from the east.[61] These plans are an indication of a perpetual panic and fear. Threats and insecurity simmer in a region whose people have never trusted Israel and its policies.

Israeli Military Barriers in the Occupied Arab Territories

Bar-Lev Line: The End of a Myth

After capturing the Sinai Peninsula from Egypt in the 1967 Six-Day War, Israel built a sand barrier, called the Bar-Lev Line, along the eastern bank of the Suez Canal covering a distance of 170 kilometers. Israel sought to achieve three key goals through the Bar-Lev Line: first, to maintain the military gains and geo-strategic position resulting from the 1967 war; second, to prevent any major Egyptian attack across the canal by erecting a sand wall that made the canal impassable by amphibious vehicles (without destroying the barrier); and third, to monitor Egyptian military activities on the western bank of the canal.

The Bar-Lev line, which Moshe Dayan, former Israeli Minister of Defense, once referred to as "one of the best anti-tank ditches in the world",[62] was in fact a complete military system. It was composed of 31

---

60   Clyde R. Mark, "Israel's Security Fences, Separating Israel from the Palestinians", CRS Report for Congress (1 August 2003), CRS-2, https://digital.library.unt.edu/ark:/67531/metacrs7718/m1/1/high_res_d/RS21564_2003Aug01.pdf

61   Herb Keinon, "P.M. Sets Summer as Completion Date for Egypt Fence", *Jerusalem Post* (15 March 2011), http://www.jpost.com/Defense/PM-sets-summer-2012-as-completion-date-for-Egypt-fence

62   Cited by George W. Gawrych, "The 1973 Arab-Israeli War: The Albatross of Decisive", *Leavenworth Papers*, No. 21 [U.S. Army Center of Military History, Washington] (1996); p. 16.

complex, multi-level strongholds that were each fortified with several reinforced-concrete bunkers that provided all round firing positions.[63] Each fortress was staffed by more than 50 soldiers who were armed with anti-tank weapons, mortars, tanks and heavy machine guns.[64] The sand wall was also equipped with wire entanglements and mine fields surrounded each fortification point that extended to a depth of 800 meters. Some points were equipped with napalm tanks giving the ability to cover the canal locally with fuel which would produce a sheet of flames one meter in height and raise the temperature of the water to boiling point.[65] The construction of the Bar-Lev Line, excluding maintenance expenses, cost nearly USD 300 million.

The major dilemma faced by the Egyptian forces, when they decided to reclaim the Sinai Peninsula, was how to destroy the Bar-Lev Line. In 1971, a young Egyptian engineer officer suggested a simple yet ingenious solution: open gaps in the sand wall by using water pumps. The Egyptian Corps of Engineers combined special British and German pumps and improved them so as to effect gaps in the wall in a three-to-five hour period. During the October 1973 war,[66] Egyptian forces surprised Israeli forces by making sixty huge gaps in the sand wall and overrunning the Bar-Lev Line. Instead of controlling Egyptian forces and preventing them from crossing the Suez Canal, the wall prevented Israeli forces from seeing the Egyptian attack.[67] Most military analysts agree that the surprise attack launched by Egypt using innovative warfare tactics and Israel's miscalculation regarding the effectiveness of the sand wall were the key elements that allowed Egyptian forces to destroy the Bar-Lev Line, which had been invincible barrier in the Israeli imagination.

---

63   Riad Ashkar, "The Syrian and Egyptian Campaigns", *Journal of Palestine Studies*, Vol. 3, No. 2 (1974), p. 20.

64   *Ibid.*, p. 58

65   H. El-Badri, T. El-Magdoub and M. Dia El-Din Zohdy, *The Ramadan War* (Dunn Loring: T. N. Dupuy Associates, Inc., 1973), p. 7.

66   The October War, also known by Arabs as the Ramadan War and by Israeli as the Yom Kippur War, launched by Egypt and Syria against Israel on 6 October 1973 to recover Sinai Peninsula and Golan Heights, which had been captured and occupied by Israel since the 1967 Six-Day War.

67   For more information about how Egyptians destroyed the bar-Lev Line see: George W. Gawrych, "The 1973 Arab-Israeli War: The Albatross of Decisive" (1996); Sa'ad Din Shazli, "How the Egyptians Crossed the Canal", interview with Lt. General Shazli, *Journal of Palestine Studies*, Vol. 3, No. 2 (1974), pp. 163–68.

Golan Heights Fence

After its occupation of the Golan Heights in 1967, Israel built a military barrier along its *de facto* border with Syria. Intended to separate the Golan from the rest of Syria, an impenetrable fence enhanced by minefields was finally completed in 1975.[68] In addition to its military goals, Israel planned to use the barrier to increase its presence in the Golan Heights by establishing its first settlement in the region as part of the occupation. When Palestinian and Syrian protesters broke through the barrier and crossed the cease-fire line on the 2011 day of commemoration of the Nakba,[69] as a symbolic return to their homeland, the Israeli reaction was violent; soldiers shot at the protesters, killing 35.

After this, Israel planned to construct a new barbed-wire fence east of the village of Majd al-Shams to prevent Palestinian and Syrian protesters from crossing the cease-fire line in the future. The resulting fence is 8 meters high, and 4 kilometers long on the side of Majd al-Shams and extends to Quneitra. According to Israeli officials, the Israeli military has deployed new mine fields along the *de facto* border with Syria since many had failed during incidents that took place on days commemorating Nakba and Naksa (previous wars with the Arab countries).[70] Syria accused Israel of harming the residents of Majd al-Shams and taking over their lands in order to build a "racist separation fence" separating the Syrian-Druze population of the Golan Heights from their Syrian motherland.[71] In addition, the Syrian government claimed that Israel tried to create new political and security facts on the ground in order to affect future negotiation on the future of the Israeli-occupied Golan Heights.[72]

---

68 Tayseer Mara'i and Usama R. Halabi, "Life under Occupation in the Golan Heights", *Journal of Palestine Studies*, Vol. 22, No. 1 (1992), p. 81.

69 *Nakba* means "catastrophe" in Arabic. It refers to the destruction of Palestinian society and the creation of Israel in 1948 when ten thousand Palestinians were killed and 750,000 were forced into exile.

70 See letter of Syria's ambassador to the United Nations, Bashar Ja'afari, to UN Secretary-General and the permanent members of the UN Security Council on 8 August 2011. Cited in Barak Ravid, "Syria Calls on UN to Thwart Israel's 'Separation Fence' on Golan Heights", *Haaretz* (15 August 2011).

71 *Ibid.*

72 *Ibid.*

The construction of the fence was regarded at that time as a pro-active move by Israel ahead of an anticipated UN vote on Palestinian statehood in October 2011. It would prevent futher storming of the cease-fire line by Palestinian and Syrian demonstrators. During the Syrian uprising that began in mid-March 2011, Israel repaired some parts of the Golan fences.

Conclusion

The separation-barrier strategy has been a key element in the construction of the Israeli state. The fencing and heavy militarization of Israel's boundaries and the creation of security and buffer zones with Arab nations; whether in Gaza, the West Bank, Egypt, Lebanon, Syria or Jordan; are intended to perpetuate occupation and to control "the other side". This is all in order to guarantee the security of a "Jewish state" and to protect its "Jewish character". It also seeks the annexation of more Palestinian land, thereby defining unilaterally the borders of a future Palestinian State, continuing the ethnic cleansing of Palestinians from the oPt and diminishing the possibility of the creation of an independent and sovereign Palestinian state in the West Bank and Gaza by interrupting its territorial contiguity.

Despite the enormous efforts and the huge amounts of money spent on constructing these separation barriers, Israel has not achieved security. Israel is still living in a region whose peoples, whether in Palestine or neighboring countries, reject its existence and have shown over time that they cannot coexist or normalize their relations with the "Jewish state". In fact, the policy of separation not only surrounds and disperses Palestinians; it also places Israel itself in a cage of its own making.

2. Border Fencing in India[1]

Current national borders in South Asia are distinguished by two particular features: first, topographic diversity and, second, the arbitrariness by which European colonial powers delineated South-Asian boundaries and imposed their notions of the territorial state. The same applies to the Post-Soviet states in central Asia where borders have been demarcated unilaterally or artificially without considering preexisting ethnic, religious, linguistic, geographical, or economic conditions. As a result of these artificially created boundaries that engendered many territorial disputes and left large areas porous for a variety of irregular and illegal cross-border activities, the countries of the region have resorted to the construction of different types of barriers along their national borders in an attempt to resolve these problems. To fight cross-border security problems and unauthorized immigration largely resulting from the manner in which nation-state has been built in the region, some Asian governments, especially in South, Central and Southeast Asia, have built barriers along their national border as a simple solution to a complex problem.

In recent decades, Asian countries have seen a huge increase in cross-border drug trafficking. This is primarily due to the widespread production of drugs in the region. For example, Afghanistan has been for a long time the world's largest producer of opium, and it is set to remain so for the foreseeable future because of the collapse of any

---

1   This chapter is drawn, with permission from the publisher, from: "Border Fencing India: Between Colonial Legacy and Changing Security Challenges", *International Journal of Arts & Sciences*, Vol. 7, No. 5 (2016), pp. 111–24.

     https://doi.org/10.11647/OBP.0121.03

state institutions that might impede production. Some of the region's countries, such as Iran and Pakistan, are major transit routes for drug smuggling.

In addition to security aspects, the fencing of borders also stems from political reasons closely related to the way in which these international borders were drawn. Since many of these borders were not defined by natural landmarks, they are often easy to cross and, since they were artificially put in place and not based on a sense of cultural identity, their legitimacy is often disputed. Hence, due to border disagreements between Asian countries, fencing can also be seen as a unilateral effort to quite literally concretize these borders as *de facto* demarcation lines. On the other hand, some of the erected fences revive long-standing territorial disputes, especially in the Indian subcontinent.

Asian countries can be divided into two groups regarding the reasons and purposes informing the construction of land demarcations: barrier-building countries (India, Iran, Uzbekistan, China, Malaysia and Thailand) and targeted countries (Afghanistan, Bangladesh, Pakistan, Myanmar, North Korea and Kyrgyzstan). If Pakistan carries out the project of fencing its border with Afghanistan, Pakistan will be at the same time a barrier-building and a targeted country.

Like all boundaries in South Asia, India's boundaries are also man-made[2] and, as they do not clearly reflect the ethnic and geographical realities on the ground, they have led to a number of political and territorial disputes with neighboring countries.

India has 15,106 kilometers of land borders and a coastline of about 7,516 kilometers. Only 5 out of 29 Indian states have no international border or coastal line. Those long borders are shared with seven countries — China, Pakistan, Bhutan, Myanmar, Afghanistan, Nepal and Bangladesh. Such extensive and porous borders run through different kinds of terrain, including mountains, hills, plains, valleys, forest, desert and swamp, and are sometimes difficult to monitor, especially at a time when territorial disputes and security troubles still plague parts of the Indian borderline.

The situation of India's boundaries is made more complex by the fact that its maritime boundaries are shared with seven countries

---

2   Pushpita Das (Ed.), *India's Border Management: Select Documents*, p. 1.

— Pakistan, Maldives, Sri Lanka, Indonesia, Thailand, Myanmar and Bangladesh. With the exception of Pakistan and Bangladesh, India has ratified all its maritime borders with adjoining countries in bilateral agreements.

I divide this chapter into two main sections: the first discusses the complex situation of India's borderline, and the second deals with the country's strategy of fencing borders with some its neighbors.

Indian Borders between Colonial Legacy and Complex Cultural Makeup

Indian borders can be divided into three categories according to their vulnerability and the manner in which they have been drawn. History, culture and religion played a significant role in defining Indian borderlines: the first category generated from the separation movements because of cultural and religious reasons like Indo-Bangladesh and Indo-Pakistan borders. Some important parts of those borders are still disputed. The second, exemplified by the Indo-Chinese boundary, resulted from reciprocal invasions and reflect regional competition for influence and power. The third category is inherited from the colonial period and includes the Indian borders with Myanmar, Bhutan and Nepal. The latter borderline, which was established by bilateral agreement, remains peaceful to this day.

India-Bangladesh and India-Pakistan Borders: Territorial Disputes and Cultural Misunderstandings

India-Bangladesh Border

The 4,096.7 kilometers long Indo-Bangladesh border is the longest land borderline that India shares with any of its neighbors. In spite of the efforts made in the last four decades, since the secession of East Pakistan (now Bangladesh) in 1971, to demarcate the entire Indo-Bangladesh border, 6.5 kilometers remain disputed. In June 2015, the governments of the two countries exchanged instruments of ratification to make operational the 1974 Land Boundary Agreement, which was unanimously passed by the Indian parliament on May 7, 2015, marking a high point in the history of India-Bangladesh relations. The main issues had included the vague demarcation of the border and the arbitrary division of the land which resulted in Bangladesh being surrounded by India on three sides (east, north and west). The border enclaves resulting from this partition had been a significant obstacle in strengthening bilateral relations and a long-standing cause of the escalating tension between the two neighbors until the problem of these enclaves was settled in 2015.[3] More importantly, the artificial delineation of the border had severely affected the traditional life of the local population who found themselves cut off from their relatives, traditional markets, agricultural land, medical facilities, etc.

The India-Bangladesh border is not the result of geographical or historical realities, but rather it reflects political and religious concerns. The partition of the Indian subcontinent in 1947 divided the population according to their religion. The secession of Pakistan — both east and west — was meant to create a state with a majority Muslim population, a goal that hasn't been fully achieved because of the ethnic and religious communities overlapping the border and existing inside the new states. According to the 2011 Census of India, Muslims constitute 14.2 percent of India's population with about 172 million adherents,[4] whereas Hindus makes up about 8.2 percent of the Bengladeshi population according to the Bangladesh Bureau of Statistics.[5]

The Indo-Bangladesh border is generally marked by three different topographies: flat/plain, riverine, and hilly/jungle with virtually no

---

3   On 6 June 2015, the two countries signed a historical agreement to exchange those enclaves and allow people living in border enclaves to choose whether to reside in India or Bangladesh. There existed 51 Bangladeshi enclaves in Indian Territory and around 111 Indian enclaves inside Bangladesh. In 1974, the two countries signed a Land and Boundary Agreement in New Delhi to demarcate the border and prevent border conflicts. According to the agreement, these enclaves were to be exchanged except for Berubari, Angarpota and Dahagram. See Harun Ur. Rashid, *Indo-Bangladesh Relations: An Insider's View*. New Delhi: Har-Anand Publications, 2002, p. 119.

4   Office of the Registrar General & Census Commissioner, India, Ministry of Home Affairs, Government of India, "2011 Census Data", http://www.censusindia.gov. in/2011-Common/CensusData2011.html

5   "Population and Housing Census 2011: Socio-economic and Demographic Report", Bangladesh Bureau of Statistics (BBS), Statistics and Informatics Division (SID), Ministry of Planning, National Series, Vol. 4 (December 2012), http://203.112.218.66/ WebTestApplication/userfiles/Image/BBS/Socio_Economic.pdf

natural boundaries between the two countries.[6] This configuration, coupled with the porosity and length of the boundary, facilitates the irregular movement of people across the border, especially from Bangladesh, which is the main source of illegal immigrants in India. The type of settlements peppering the border represents a further challenge for India's border surveillance as the boundary cuts through several heavily populated villages and even bisects some houses.[7] Indians and Bangladeshis live side by side along the borderline separating the two countries and imposed. The high permeability of the India-Bangladesh border results in a diverse immigration flow mostly from Bangladesh to India, comprising unauthorized immigrants, refugees, and people displaced by climate. Each year, many Bangladeshis cross into India seeking employment and improved living standards, fleeing harsh environmental conditions, or escaping political and religious persecution, a situation which poses major challenges to the Indian government.

India-Pakistan Border

Similar to its boundary with Bangladesh, India shares a 3,325-kilometer border with Pakistan that runs through a diverse terrain which also facilitates illegal cross-border movement and smuggling activities in villages adjacent to the border.[8] Mahmud A. Durrani, an academic and retired Pakistan Major General, distinguishes between four categories of the Pakistan-India border:[9] the first is the international border, also known as the "Radcliffe line", which is about 2,200 kilometers long and was officially recognized by the two countries in August 1947. This line defines the border between the Pakistani and Indian provinces of Punjab in the north and the Sir Creek in the south. The

---

6   N. S. Jamwal, "Border Management: Dilemma of Guarding the India-Bangladesh Border", *Strategic Analysis*, Vol. 28, No. 1 (2004), p. 8.

7   *Ibid.*, p. 9.

8   Pushpita Das (Ed.), *India's Border Management: Select Documents*, p. 11.

9   Mahmud Ali Durrani, "Enhancing Security through a Cooperative Border Monitoring Experiment: A Proposal for India and Pakistan", Cooperative Monitoring Center, Occasional Paper 21 (July 2001), p. 26. See also the following Pushpita Das book who distinguishes between three different categories of Indo-Pak border. Pushpita Das (Ed.), *India's Border Management: Select Documents*, pp. 10–11.

second type, the Working Boundary which is recognized by India as an international border, comprises the 200 kilometer-long borderline between the old Indian states of Jammu and Kashmir and Pakistan's Punjab. The third boundary, the Line of Control (LoC) or the Ceasefire Line (CFL), is about 767 kilometers long and divides the former princely state of Kashmir into two areas — the Pakistan-controlled and the Indian-controlled regions. The fourth type of borderline, the Line of Contact (Holding), is about 95 kilometers long and represents the line of contact between the Indian and Pakistani troops fighting along the Siachen glacier.[10]

The border between India and Pakistan is the most sensitive of India's borders because of the dispute over Kashmir[11] which started with its annexation by India in 1947. Since then the region has fuelled a bitter dispute between the two countries. In 1954, upon India's announcement that its accession of the region was final, the Ceasfire Line (CFL) established in 1949 that cuts through Kashmir, became the *de facto* border between the two states.[12] Since then, India has tried a number of measures to consolidate this annexation, including erecting fences to fortify the borderline with Pakistan. Yet, this area still represents the most militarily active border in India, having been the site of three wars and one near war.

Since the partition of the sub-continent in 1947, the instability on the India-Pakistan border has soured relations between the two countries and fuelled a relentless conflict over the Kashmir region. As both India and Pakistan possess nuclear weapons and thus have the military capability to wipe each other out, the Indian subcontinent is one of the most unstable regions in the world and the dispute over Kashmir poses a constant threat of sparking an armed conflict between the two countries.

---

10 Mahmud Ali Durrani, "Enhancing Security through a Cooperative Border Monitoring Experiment: A Proposal for India and Pakistan".

11 Rick "Ozzie" Nelson (dir.), "Border Security in a Time of Transformation: Two International Case Studies—Poland and India", A Report of the CSIS Homeland Security & Counterterrorism Program, Europe Program, and South Asia Program (July 2010), http://csis.org/files/publication/100709_Nelson_BorderSecurity_web.pdf

12 Rajat Ganguly, "India, Pakistan and the Kashmir Dispute", working paper, Asian Studies Institute (1998), p. 3.

India-China Border: A Fault Line between Two Regional Powers

Although India gained its independence in 1947, it had not shared a common boundary with China until 1950 when China annexed Tibet, which was seen as a political buffer between the two countries. Since then, the entire India-China border, which extends for 3,488 kilometers, is still disputed because China has not yet recognized the controversial McMahon Line.[13] The McMahon Line was drawn in 1914 to delineate the boundary Between Tibet and British India. It is recognized by India as the international border, whereas China rejects this demarcation line and claims the eastern Himalayas which is administered by India. This territorial dispute between India and China escalated in the 1950s and resulted in the 1962 war between the two countries, which ended with a new *status quo* border known as Line of Actual Control (LAC) that separates India from China-Tibet. As the LAC has never been delimited and due to increasing mistrust of China after the 1962 conflict, India moved towards closer relations with the U.S. and armed itself with nuclear weapons.

Because of the lack of people and goods flowing across the Chinese-Indian boundary, the management of this disputed border does not pose serious challenges to the two countries. Therefore, the erection of a fence along this border may not be on the table. Moreover, the Himalayan Mountains are natural barriers preventing significant cross-border interaction in the region.

India and China have had little political interaction throughout most of their history despite their geographical proximity. The tensions between the two nations have increased because of the dispute over the Tibet border region and escalated owing to their competing strategies and ambitions in South Asia. Given the strategic importance of the region, the two neighboring giants are expected to be in constant competition for regional leadership. Moreover, rising demand from the two countries for natural resources and energy due to their rapid industrialization and economic growth over the last two decades leads them further into competition, especially in Africa where Chinese and Indian companies are both investing more and more. The challenge is

---

13   Pushpita Das (Ed.), *India's Border Management: Select Documents*, p. 40.

that the two countries are competing for the same resources and on the same battlefields. On the other hand, India and China have common interests in the management of international economic and financial systems. As reflected in the creation of the BRICS group, they have shown themselves to be willing to mitigate their disagreements and combine efforts with other developing countries.

India-Myanmar, India-Nepal and India-Bhutan Borders: Quiet and Stable

India-Myanmar Border

India and Myanmar share a 1,640-kilometer land border and a long maritime border in the Andaman Sea and the Bay of Bengal. The two borders were delimited and demarcated by two bilateral agreements: the land-boundary agreement signed on 10 March 1967 and ratified shortly thereafter and the maritime-boundary agreement of 1982. The India-Myanmar border, like other international Indian sub-continental frontiers, is characterized by high porosity. Additionally, the India-Myanmar border topography varies from low mountains in the south to high ridges and peaks in the north, adjacent to the Himalaya. As a result, unlike the India-Bangladesh borderland, the region is one of low population density.[14]

As Pushpita Das points out, the India-Myanmar border is highly vulnerable due to a number of factors. First, the boundary has not yet been concretized on the ground as lines separating two sovereign countries. Second, the border traverses a region in which numerous insurgencies operate. Thirdly, the India-Myanmar border has a unique arrangement in a place called the Free Movement Regime, which permits the tribes residing along the border to travel 16 kilometers across the boundary without visa restrictions. This place becomes a safe haven for different illegal activities like drug smuggling, human trafficking, infiltration

---

14   U.S. State Department, Bureau of Intelligence and Research, "Burma-India Boundary", *International Boundary Study*, No. 80 (15 May 1968), p. 2.

and cross-border movements of insurgents. Finally, there is inadequate management of this border by India.[15]

Indo-Nepal Border

The Nepal-India boundary, which runs along the west, south and east of Nepal, is 1,580 kilometers long and dates back to the Anglo-Nepal War of 1814–1876. The Nepal-India border has been open since 1950 when the two neighboring countries signed the Nepal-India Peace and Friendship Treaty.[16] The unrestricted movement of people across this border over the centuries has enhanced social and cultural ties and expanded economic and political interdependence between the two countries' people,[17] who share many commonalities. Although there are many border disputes which have not yet been resolved, the special relationship between the two countries is not seriously affected, and the movement of their people is allowed throughout the borderline.

Indo-Bhutan Border

Although the demarcation process of the 669-kilometer long India-Bhutan border took from 1961 to 2006 to establish, it is now one of the two most stable of India's borders (the other being its border with Nepal). With the exception of a small part along the tri-junction with China, the entire India-Bhutan border is now officially demarcated.[18] Bhutan is surrounded by China and India. Since its border with China is still closed because disputed territory and the absence of diplomatic relations,[19] India remains the only route for Bhutan to access the outside world.

---

15 Pushpita Das, „India-Myanmar Border Problems: Fencing Not the Only Solution", Institute for Defence Studies and Analyses (15 November 2013), http://www.idsa.in/idsacomments/IndiaMyanmarBorderProblems_pdas_151113.html

16 Vidya Bir Singh Kansakar, "Nepal-India Open Border: Prospects, Problems and Challenges", *Institute of Foreign Affairs* [Kathmandu, Nepal] (2001), http://www.fes.de/aktuell/focus_interkulturelles/focus_1/documents/19.pdf

17 Pushpita Das (Ed.), *India's Border Management: Select Documents*, p. 6.

18 *Ibid.*, p. 8.

19 Bhutan is the only one of China's 14 neighbors with which it doesn't have diplomatic relations.

The Fencing of the Indian Borders: One Policy and Different Contexts

The common denominator that characterizes India's border barriers is their material composition. Almost all of these barriers are made up of barbed-wire fence. Compared to most other cases, including Israeli barriers, the U.S.-Mexico border fence and fences of Ceuta and Melilla, the Indian border barriers are, in general, low tech and low cost.

Despite a diversity of goals targeted by the Indian border-fencing policy, security concerns are the top priority for its border-control systems. Security concerns encompass a wide range of illegal infiltration, including insurgency activities, terrorism, drug trafficking and organized crime. Preventing unauthorized crossings, especially those by undocumented immigrants, is the second most important purpose of the Indian border-fencing policy. The porosity of its borders and the existence of some border tribes within more than one adjacent country make India's border control extremely challenging. Additionally, disputes over border demarcation have complicated the construction of fences in some instances. The effect of territorial disputes on the construction of border fences are clearly seen on India's border with Pakistan and Bangladesh, where political concerns remain the key determinant of India's border-fencing policy.

It is difficult to classify India's border barriers into specific groups with similar characteristics because they were built within such different contexts and with differing goals. Of the large number of cases I have studied, few have much in common so each shall be addressed separately.

Fencing of the Indo-Bangladesh Border

The idea of fencing off the Indo-Bangladesh boundary dates back to the 1960s when some politicians in the Assam region proposed erecting a fence along its length in order to isolate the population of East Pakistan (now Bangladesh).[20] This plan was to be executed in conjunction with a

---

20   Jolin Joseph and Vishnu Narendran, "Neither Here nor There: An Overview of South-South Migration from both ends of the Bangladesh-India Migration Corridor", working paper No. 569, *Migration Literature Review*, No. 1 (October 2013), p. 20.

campaign launched by the Government of Assam to deport Bangladeshis settled in the region.[21]

Although some Islamic groups have used its porous eastern border with Bangladesh in recent years to enter India and carry out bombings, security is a minor factor in defining its fencing policy along the border with Bangladesh. Other factors, particularly the unauthorized flow of immigration, were a greater concern. Consequently, India took the decision in 1986 to fence off the entire Indo-Bangladesh border,[22] which became the central component of India's "border management strategy" — a collection of policies and practices aimed at "hardening" the border and enclosing Indian territory on its eastern periphery.[23] In 1989, the Government of India initiated the first phase of building its border with Bangladesh, resulting in the erection of about 854 kilometers of fencing, almost 20 percent of the border.[24] In 2000, India sanctioned phase two, which targeted the fencing of a further 2,430 kilometers. By 31 January 2005, 1,275 kilometers — about half — had been completed.[25] In addition to fencing, India has also constructed a series of roads along its border with Bangladesh to facilitate the monitoring of operations. So far, roads stretching approximately 2,866 kilometers have been completed as part of phase one[26] and about 2,800 kilometers of border roads and 24 kilometers of bridges are expected to be built under phase two in the states of West

21 Sanjoy Hazarika, Rites of Passage: Border Crossings, Imagined Homelands, India's East and Bangladesh. New Delhi: Penguin Books, 2000, p. 117.

22 Sreeradha Datta, "Security of India's Northeast: External Linkages", *Strategic Analysis*, Vol. 24, No. 8 (2000), p. 1503.

23 Duncan McDuie-Ra, "Tribals, Migrants and Insurgents: Security and Insecurity along the India-Bangladesh Border", *Global Change, Peace & Security*, Vol. 24, No. 1 (2012), p. 165.

24 Rizwana Shamshad, "Politics and Origin of the Indian-Bangladesh Border Fence", paper presented to the 17th Biennial Conference of the Asian Studies Association of Australia, Melbourne (1–3 July 2008), p. 9; Pushpita Das. "The India-Bangladesh Border: A Problem Area for Tomorrow", working paper, Institute for Defence Studies and Analyses, New Delhi, India (8 December 2006), http://www.idsa.in/idsastrategiccomments/TheIndiaBangladeshBorder AProblemAreaforTomorrow_PDas_081206

25 N. S. Jamwal, "Border Management: Dilemma of Guarding the India-Bangladesh Border", *Strategic Analysis*, Vol. 28, No. 1 (2004), p. 22; see also Pushpita Das, "The India-Bangladesh Border: A Problem Area for Tomorrow" (8 December 2006).

26 *Ibid.*

Bengal, Assam, Meghalaya, Tripura and Mizoram.[27] The Indian Ministry of Home Affairs has admitted that most of the fence constructed in the first phase in West Bengal, Assam, and Meghalaya has been damaged due to adverse climatic conditions, notably by repeated submergence.[28] Accordingly, the government of India has sanctioned a third phase of construction that would replace 861 kilometers of fencing originally built in phase one;[29] 532 kilometers of fencing has been replaced so far. The scheduled completion date for the entire project was March 2010,[30] however, the India-Bangladesh border had not yet been entirely fenced off. The project has not been fully realized because of land-acquisition issues, public reactions, and inclement weather conditions. In 2014, the Indian Ministry of Home Affairs revised its deadline to complete fencing along the India-Bangladesh border by March 2012.[31]

Fig. 2.1 Indo-Bangladesh Barrier (29 December 2007).
Photo by Nicolas Merky, CC BY-SA 3.0.[32]

---

27 Willem van Schendel, *The Bengal Borderland: Beyond State and Nation in South Asia*. London: Anthem Press, 2005, p. 237.

28 Government of India, Ministry of Home Affairs, *Annual Report 2007–2008*, p. 30, http://www.satp.org/satporgtp/countries/india/document/papers/annualreport_2007-08.htm

29 Government of India, Ministry of Home Affairs, *Annual Report 2009–2010*, p. 30, https://www.mea.gov.in/Uploads/PublicationDocs/171_Annual-Report-2009-2010.pdf

30 *Ibid.*

31 "Fenced Border by 2014, Says Delhi", *The Telegraph* (29 April 2013), http://www.telegraphindia.com/1130429/jsp/northeast/story_16839610.jsp#.UzdHlYXuiRo

32 Source: Wikimedia Commons, https://commons.wikimedia.org/wiki/File%3AIndo-Bangladeshi_Barrier.JPG

While some of the disputes on the interpretation and implementation of India-Bangladesh boundary have been solved, many still exist.[33] Although the Indian government considers the fence as a "protective device" to prevent the influx of illegal migrants across the border, the Bangladeshi government has strongly rejected this justification. It cites the India-Bangladesh Agreement of 1975 which clearly prohibits the construction of any "defensive structure" of any kind or the deployment of any permanent or temporary border-security forces by either country in their respective territories within 150 yards of the border.[34] Moreover, the Bangladeshi government claimed that the fences intruded into Bangladeshi territory at several points and constituted an attempt to appropriate its territory.[35]

In order to mitigate disputes between the two countries arising from the fencing project, they signed a series of agreements in 2011 aimed at reaching a common vision about the management of their border. First, in March 2011, they agreed to disallow the Border Security Force to use lethal weapons. Then, both sides signed the Coordinated Border Management Plan in July 2011 and the Protocol to the Agreement Concerning the Demarcation of Land Boundary in September 2011. Such accords are expected to transform the India-Bangladesh border from a border-management nightmare to a zone of peace and prosperity.[36]

Mehrotra-Khanna (2005) identified some major reasons that have rendered the India-Bangladesh border management ineffective, citing the incoherence of security personnel system, the fragility and inefficiency of different forces in charge of border control and the porosity of the frontier. She concluded that these difficulties have kept the borders vulnerable and have, in turn, facilitated problems of

---

33 N. S. Jamwal, "Border Management: Dilemma of Guarding the India- Bangladesh Border", *Strategic Analysis*, Vol. 28, No. 1 (2004), p. 5.

34 Hiranmay Karlekar, *Bangladesh: The Next Afghanistan?* New Delhi: Sage Publication, 2005, p. 88. See also N. S. Jamwal "Border Management: Dilemma of Guarding the India- Bangladesh Border", p. 30.

35 V.K. Vinayaraj, "India as a Threat: Bangladesh Perceptions", *South Asian Survey*, Vol. 16, No. 1 (2009), p. 107.

36 Pushpita Das, "The India-Bangladesh Border: A Problem Area for Tomorrow" (8 December 2006).

illegal infiltration, smuggling and trafficking.[37] So, although fencing has undoubtedly made infiltration more difficult, it cannot end it.[38] Smugglers and undocumented migrants have invented new ways to bypass the border security systems, including cutting the barbed wire. Additionally, the two countries share almost 200 kilometers of river border, mostly in Dhubri district of Assam and southern West Bengal, which is impossible to fence off.

In relation to the demographic composition and distribution on the India-Bangladesh borderland, fencing the border cannot be effective in checking infiltration and stopping unauthorized cross-border activities while each country has many enclaves and adverse possessions inside the other. This situation is expected to end after the 1974 Land Boundary Agreement (LBA) was finally ratified by both India and Bangladesh in June 2015. The governments of the two countries sealed the ratification pact to operationalize the LBA and exchange the enclaves.

The arbitrary and artificial nature of the Indo-Bangladesh border has been reflected in India's security control and fencing strategy along this boundary. The erection of fencing has stopped or been delayed in the areas of 450 villages located within 150 yards of the border. Here, the construction of defensive structures or the deployment of security fences has been precluded by the 1975 Indo-Bangladesh border agreement.[39] Additionally, no fewer than 200 border villages oppose the fence. In some border areas, like Hilli in the Malda district of West Bengal, a row of houses have their front doors in India and their rear doors opening into Bangladesh.[40] The barbed-wire fence not only affects the social and economic life of the population and makes them refugees in their motherland but perpetuates the arbitrary nature of the border delineation.

---

37 Mansi Mehrotra-Khanna, "Security Challenges to India-Bangladesh Relations", working paper, Center for Land Warfare Studies (2010), p. 24.

38 Praveen Swami, "Failed Threats and Flawed Fences: India's Military Responses to Pakistan's Proxy War", *India Review*, Vol. 3, No. 2 (2004), p. 166.

39 Chandra Moni Bhattarai, "India-Bangladesh Border Fencing and Community Responses", conference paper, Annual International Studies Convention 2013 [Delhi, India] (10–12 December 2013).

40 Chandra Moni Bhattarai, "India-Bangladesh Border Fencing and Community Responses", conference paper, Annual International Studies Convention 2013 (10–12 December 2013).

Fencing the India-Pakistan Border

Erecting fences and installing floodlight systems are the main projects carried out by the Indian government to secure its border with Pakistan from infiltration and other illegal cross-border activities. Pakistan has always objected to India's fence constructed along the border of Jammu and Kashmir, claiming that the barrier violates the United Nations Charter and the ceasefire agreement and alters the status of the region which Pakistan considers disputed territory.

Construction of the fences began in the late 1980s in the state of Punjab when India faced an armed Sikh separatist uprising, and weapons were being smuggled from Pakistan.[41] In 1994, India pushed ahead with the construction of fences along the border of Jammu and Kashmir. The building process was stopped because of relentless Pakistani fire but resumed again along the international border in Jammu in early 2001.[42] As of November 2009, of the 2,044 kilometers identified for fencing along the India-Pakistan border, 1,916 kilometers had been completed, 1,862 kilometers had been floodlit and 148 kilometers of planned floodlighting remains to be completed.[43] Besides these methods of boundary control, the government of India began in 2007 to deploy more specialized technologies on all its international borders, including in Kashmir. It has implemented night-vision devices, hand-held thermal imagers, battlefield-surveillance radars, direction finders, unattended ground sensors, high-powered telescopes and more.[44] According to some media resources, the fence consists of three layers and is about 3.5 meters high.[45]

---

41 Rama Lakshmi, "India's Border Fence Extended to Kashmir Country Aims to Stop Pakistani Infiltration", *The Washington Post* (30 July 2003), http://antigenocide.org/images/India-30-Jul-03-India_s_Border_Fence_Extended_to_Kashmir.pdf

42 Sudha Ramachandran, "India: No sitting on the Fence", *Asia Times Online* (3 December 2003), http://www.atimes.com/atimes/South_Asia/EL03Df05.html

43 Ravinder Singh, "Fencing and Floodlighting for Better Vigil along Borders", *The Indian Post Daily News* (10 February 2010), http://www.theindiapost.com/articles/fencing-and-floodlighting-for-better-vigil-along-borders/

44 Government of India, *Annual Report 2007–2008 of the Union Ministry of Home Affairs.* New Delhi: Government of India (2008), p. 31, http://mha.nic.in/sites/upload_files/mha/files/pdf/ar0708-Eng.pdf

45 Binoo Joshi, "India-Pakistan Border Fence affecting Wildlife", *Indo-Asian News Service* (6 February 2008), http://twocircles.net/node/78400

In addition, landmines are laid along the fence as it runs from flat plains through mountainous forests.[46]

Fig. 2.2 India-Pakistan border at night (23 September 2015).
NASA Earth Observatory, public domain.[47]

The two countries seem to take opposite approaches to the Line of Control in Jammu and Kashmir. India tries to maintain the *status quo* and impose the LoC as the legal international border by erecting fences and installing advanced sensors along the Line. Pakistan, meanwhile, tries to change this situation and prevent India from formalizing the LoC through both diplomatic means and proxy war. Fenced borders between the countries, however, will not be effective without Pakistan being persuaded to collaborate with India in a joint strategy to control their common boundary. The fenced border remains a temporary solution unless the issue of Kashmir itself is resolved.

Recently, the Indian government concluded, after discovered a 400-meter-long tunnel running from Pakistan into India on 28 July 2012, that its expensive security border system, including fencing, unattended ground sensors, and other gadgets, has not worked as planned and is

---

46   *Ibid.*
47   Source: Wikimedia Commons, https://commons.wikimedia.org/wiki/File:India-Pakistan_Border_at_Night.jpg

not sufficient to monitor the country's porous border. Accordingly, the Indian Home Ministry plans to build advanced structures to manage the country's more than 15,000-kilometer border with China, Pakistan, Bangladesh, Nepal and Myanmar. The new system will use satellite technology and will cost more than USD 2 billion in subsequent years to manage the border.

Detecting the infiltration of Kashmiri dissidents and preventing them from carrying out attacks, whether in India or Jammu and Kashmir, remains the main reason for the building of the security fence along India's *de facto* border with Pakistan. So, military and security objectives are the major determining factor in fencing and militarizing the India-Pakistan border. Other stated goals, such as the prevention of undocumented immigration and drug trafficking, are negligible.

It is worth mentioning that a decline of cross-border infiltration in Jammu and Kashmir has been noted since 2004. This is the result of not only the fencing but of political rapprochement between India and Pakistan in the last decade. Rampant corruption in border crossing and "innovative methods" used by those who cross the Indo-Pakistani border are likely to sustain illegal cross-border activities.[48] The porosity of the Line of Control and its diverse geographical terrains and dense forests in some areas limit the effectiveness of the fence. Furthermore, fences cannot be erected in the high mountains in which the two neighbors could deploy some measures of cooperative monitoring.

Fencing the Myanmar-India Border

In 2003, India and Myanmar carried out a detailed survey of fencing along the international border for militancy and drug trafficking.[49] By the end of 2006, a 400-kilometer border with Myanmar was already fenced and was being extended in height. In addition, a stretch of 14 kilometers near the international boundary at the border town of Moreh was identified for fencing.[50] Due to recent increases in militant activities,

---

48   D. Suba Chandran and P.G. Rajamohan, "Soft, Porous or Rigid? Towards Stable Borders in South Asia", *South Asian Survey*, Vol. 14, No. 1 (2007), p. 125.

49   "India, Burma to Fence the Border", *Mizzima News* (17 May 2003), http://www. burmalibrary.org/TinKyi/archives/2003-05/msg00018.html

50   C. S. Kuppuswamy, "Indo-Myanmar Relations—A Review", working paper No. 2043, South Asia Analysis Group (November 2006).

the Government of India has decided to fence the area between BP No. 79 and 81 along the Indo-Myanma Border.[51] The last section of the fence has drastically affected the traditional life of many villages located along the Myanmar border and is likely to cause serious disturbance to migratory habits of wild animals and upset their breeding cycles.[52]

India was primarily motivated to fence a large part of its border with Myanmar in order to stop irregular immigration and human trafficking and to disrupt the flourishing narcotic trade. The United Nations Office on Drugs and Crime (UNODC) has found that Myanmar is the second largest country for the cultivation of opium poppies (17 percent of global cultivation).[53] India has traditionally been an important consumer of opium,[54] the majority of which originates in Myanmar.[55] The latter ranks fourth of the countries in East and South-East Asia that are most frequently cited as a source of methamphetamine.[56]

According to some Indian officials,[57] one of the main goals aimed at by fencing the India-Myanmar border (especially in Manipur province, a state in north-eastern India) is to check the free movement of separatist rebels and new recruits to their base camps in the no-man's-land between the two countries. Dissident movements and organized crime groups finance their activities by smuggling drugs into India in exchange for arms and ammunition and also to pay for the training of their cadres in camps run by other outfits.[58] The UNODC reported in

51   Indian Ministry of Home Affairs, *Annual Report 2009–2010*, p. 42, http://mha.nic.in/sites/upload_files/mha/files/pdf/AR(E)0910.pdf

52   "Border Fencing upsets Village Life in Moreh", *The Sangai Express* (9 May 2011), http://e-pao.net/GP.asp?src=3..100511.may11

53   UNODC, *World Drug Report 2010*. Vienna: United Nations Publication, 2010, p. 137, https://www.unodc.org/documents/wdr/WDR_2010/World_Drug_Report_2010_lo-res.pdf

54   UNODC, "A Century of International Drug Control", 2008, p. 15, cited in UNODC, *World Drug Report 2010*, p. 40, https://www.unodc.org/documents/wdr/WDR_2010/World_Drug_Report_2010_lo-res.pdf

55   UNODC, *World Drug Report 2010*, p. 41, https://www.unodc.org/documents/wdr/WDR_2010/World_Drug_Report_2010_lo-res.pdf

56   *Ibid.*, p. 114.

57   See for example the statement of the Indian Major General C. A. Krishanan, Inspector General of Assam Rifles (South India) in Iboyaima Laithangbam, "Fencing along Manipur-Myanmar Border progressing", *The Hindu* (8 September 2010), http://www.thehindu.com/news/national/article619798.ece

58   L. Kanchan, "Negotiating Insurgencies", Faultlines (11 April 2002), http://www.satp.org/satporgtp/publication/faultlines/volume11/Article7.htm; Pradip Saikia,

2010 that the processing and trafficking of opiates constitute significant sources of income for insurgents in some opium-producing countries such as Myanmar.[59]

Besides fencing the border, India has tried to cooperate with Myanmar in managing border-related issues, including countering insurgency, policing narcotics smuggling, reducing irregular immigration, sharing intelligence and organizing training for anti-narcotics officials.[60] It is noteworthy that cross-border drug trafficking in this region is not unidirectional (from Myanmar to India), rather it has grown to move in both directions. Heroin and synthetic drugs come from Myanmar to India, while chemicals like acetic anhydride and ephedrine, essential from converting raw opium into heroin, are transported from India.[61] Fences are useless and ineffective in reducing illegal cross-border activities here, mainly because of the India's long, porous and topographically hostile border with Myanmar and because of corruption among agencies responsible for border control and law enforcement.[62]

Conclusion

It is clear that the fortification and militarization of the Indian borders through the building of fences and related security measures has largely failed to achieve the desired outcomes. For that reason, the Indian government continues to pump money into the reform of existing systems or the adoption of new ones. Specific geographical characteristics of the Indian borders and the rampant corruption in

---

"North-East India as a Factor in India's Diplomatic Engagement with Myanmar: Issues and Challenges", *Strategic Analysis*, Vol. 33, No. 6 (2009), p. 881.

59   UNODC, *World Drug Report 2010*, p. 34, https://www.unodc.org/documents/wdr/WDR_2010/World_Drug_Report_2010_lo-res.pdf

60   Thin Thin Aung and Soe Myint, "India-Burma Relations", *Challenges to Democratization in Burma*. Stockholm: International Institute for Democracy and Electoral Assistance, 2001, pp. 87–96.

61   Langpoklakpam Suraj Singh, "Indo-Myanmar Relations in the Greater Perspective of India's Look East Policy: Implications on Manipur", in *Look East Policy & India's North East: Polemics and Perspectives*. Thingnam Kishan Singh (Ed.). *New Delhi*: *Concept*, 2008, p. 166; Bertil Lintner, *Burma in Revolt: Opium and Insurgency since 1948*. Boulder: Westview Press, 1994, p. 29.

62   L. S. Singh, "Indo-Myanmar Relations in the Greater Perspective of India's Look East Policy: Implications on Manipur", p. 166.

the border-patrol forces make fencing and physically managing the border in this region extremely difficult. Additionally, fencing the bilateral boundaries is complicated by disputes over the demarcation of the border. Some countries view the fencing policy led by India as a unilateral demarcation aimed at imposing *de facto* borders.

Although the security challenges facing India have been driven its policy of border fortification, an impetus also exists to reinforce regional cross-border cooperation. Regional economic integration can be a solution for both territorial disputes and unauthorized cross-border movements. Such integration can blur political aspects of South Asia's borders and transform them into spheres of economic and cultural interaction, especially in borderlands where local people have shared culture, heritage and resources. In other words, border-fencing strategies and related security measures will continue to be ineffective solutions against complicated and multifaceted problems such as undocumented migration and other illegal cross-border activities if a comprehensive policy is not put in place that takes into account the interests and rights of all parties.

3. The Fences of Ceuta and Melilla[1]

The fences of Ceuta and Melilla provide a model by which it is possible to study the extent to which governments' stated purposes and hidden objectives align in the establishment of territorial boundaries. The Spanish government uses the challenge of irregular immigration as an argument for reinforcing the fences of the two enclaves even though reports insist that the number of irregular immigrants crossing to Spain via these two towns or elsewhere has increased since the construction of the fences in the early 1990s. This suggests that the more border-surveillance measures are intensified, the more clandestine ways of crossing international borders will be found.

Ceuta and Melilla reflect a long history of interactions between Morocco and Spain. These relations have fluctuated between coexistence and confrontation according to changing regional circumstances and the balance of power in the Mediterranean region. A Spanish presence in North Africa can be traced to the era dominated by an intensive struggle between Christians and Muslims for territorial control not only in the Iberian Peninsula in the whole of the Western Mediterranean region. The Spanish term "Reconquista" refers to this long period between 718 to 1492 that ended with what Islamic history calls the "fall of al-Andalus". However, the ambitions of the "Reconquista" wars were not limited to the reclamation of the Iberian Peninsula only, but included the expansion of Christian control into Northwest Africa.

---

1   This chapter is drawn, with permission from the publisher, from my article, "Les clôtures de Ceuta et de Melilla: Une frontière européenne multidimensionnelle", *Études internationales*, Vol. 43, No. 1 (2012), pp. 49–65.

    https://doi.org/10.11647/OBP.0121.04

Ceuta and Melilla are two of the most important Spanish-controlled enclaves in Northern Morocco following the end of "Reconquista". Melilla was the first to fall under Spanish rule in 1497, and Ceuta, which had been seized by Portugal in 1415, was transferred to Spain under the Treaty of Lisbon in 1668. Ceuta and Melilla, like all medieval cities, were surrounded by high and thick stone walls to protect and defend them from invaders and all kinds of external attacks. Both towns had been longstanding epicenters for the conflict between Mediterranean powers. As a principal defensive strategy of the old-world order, the ancient walls had not been a disputed issue between Morocco and Spain. Building new fences and extending or renovating the existing ones on the border of the two enclaves today, however, has provoked political and juridical differences to emerge between the two countries.

Apart from Ceuta and Melilla, Spain controls a few small islands[2] that are considered by Morocco for historical and geographical reasons to be integral parts of its territory.

The year 1986 was a turning point in the history of the two towns and other islands controlled by Spain in Northern Morocco. As part of Spain's entry into the European Economic Community (later, the European Union), they also became EU territories.

A remarkable development occurred in these territories in 1993 when, under the pretext of preventing irregular immigration, these enclaves' perimeters began to be marked by fences. As these initial fences were relatively easy to cross, the construction of a more secure system was begun in autumn 1995.[3] From that time, the Spanish government has continued to reinforce the fences physically and through the use of advanced technologies, like infrared cameras.

In 2005, the Spanish government built a third fence next to the two deteriorated ones already in place, in order to completely seal the border from penetration apart from at designated checkpoints. The European Union contributed financially to the project, introducing a new dynamic.

---

2   Morocco's rocky islands still under Spain's control, or in a *status quo*, are: the Chafarine Islands (las Islas Chafarinas), Badis Peninsula (Peñón de Vélez de la Gomera), Nekor Island (Peñón de Alhucemas), and the Parsley Island (known also as la Isla Perejil, Tura or Laela).

3   Stefan Alscher, "Knocking at the Doors of 'Fortress Europe': Immigration and Border Control in Southern Spain and Eastern Poland", working paper No. 126, Humboldt University, Berlin, Germany (November 2005), p. 10.

It gave £200 million for the construction of the razor-wire border fence around Ceuta, and it assumed 75 percent of the costs of the first project from 1995 to 2000.

Fig. 3.1 Map of Ceuta and Melilla in Northern Morocco, three screenshots from Google Maps. © 2017 Google, all rights reserved.[4]

The current situation of the two towns' fences, according to a report made by the European Commission in October 2005, is as follows:

The external land border of Melilla is characterized by an approximately 10.5-kilometer double-border fence divided into three sectors. The outer fence has a height of 3.5 metres; the inner fence reaches 6 metres in some places. Both fences are equipped with barbed wire in order to prevent irregular immigrants from climbing the fence. The installed surveillance system consists of 106 fixed cameras for video surveillance and an additional microphone cable as well as infrared surveillance.[5]

---

4   Map data © 2017 Google.
5   European Commission. "Technical Mission to Morocco. Visit to Ceuta and Melilla on Illegal Immigration", Mission Report (October 7–11, 2005), p. 70, http://www.migreurop.org/IMG/pdf/rapport-ceuta-melilla-2.pdf

Fig. 3.2 Fence of Melilla (28 February 2009).
Photo by Miguel González Novo, CC BY-SA 2.0.[6]

Fig. 3.3. Fence of Ceuta (15 June 2012).
Photo by Mario Sánchez Bueno, CC BY-SA 2.0.[7]

---

6   Source: Wikimedia Commons, https://commons.wikimedia.org/wiki/File%3A
     Garita_de_vigilancia_en_la_frontera_de_Melilla.jpg
7   Source: Wikimedia Commons, https://commons.wikimedia.org/wiki/File%3A
     Ceuta_border_fence.jpg

At the external land border of Ceuta (a 7.8 kilometer-long, double-border fence, divided into three sectors) 316 policemen and 626 Guardia Civil officers are currently deployed. Except for 37 installed movable cameras along this border line, the technical equipment used for border surveillance is the same as in Melilla. In addition, helicopters are used for surveillance of the external border after the recent massive attacks.[8]

Pursuing a strategy of separating Spanish-controlled enclaves in North Africa from Moroccan territory, the Spanish government allocated in the beginning of 2009 an important budget to renovate and strengthen razor-wire fences surrounding Ceuta and Melilla.

In addition to these to two physical fences, the digital surveillance of irregular immigration is now a central part of the Spanish government's policy. The Integrated System of External Surveillance (SIVE)[9] is one of the largest surveillance systems in Europe aimed at monitoring the Spanish maritime areas targeted by irregular immigrants. The SIVE was first applied in 1999 around the strait of Gibraltar, where the majority of irregular immigrants were arriving at that time. The Spanish government has subsequently extended the SIVE to the east and to the west to cover respectively the whole of Cadiz province in 2004, the entire Andalusia coast in 2005, and, finally, the Canary Islands. The SIVE has been implemented through the gradual addition of border-control and -management technologies, including long-distance radar systems, advanced sensors that can detect heartbeats from a distance, thermal cameras, night vision cameras, infrared optics, helicopters and patrol boats.

Spain's virtual fence, similarly to the American one, required a large budget funded partly by the EU. For the period 1999 to 2004, the SIVE was allocated 150 million euros, which translated into about 1,800 euros per immigrant intercepted during the five-year period in question.[10] This elevated cost was justified by the necessity to adapt to the standards demanded by the EU.[11] Despite the high financial and logistical costs, Spain's virtual-fence system has not achieved significant results in preventing irregular immigrants from risking their lives by

---

8   *Ibid.*

9   Sistema Integrado de Vigilancia Exterior.

10   Jørgen Carling, "Migration Control and Migrant Fatalities at the Spanish-African Borders", *International Migration Review*, Vol. 41, No. 2 (2007), p. 325.

11   As the former Spain's Minister of the Interior, Jaime Mayor Oreja, stated in a comment on the program.

sailing across the Mediterranean and the Atlantic Ocean on rickety boats from remote western African beaches in Senegal and Mauritania. Jørgen Carling argued that the development of SIVE has not only led smugglers to adopt new routes but has also resulted in technical and organizational changes on the part of the smugglers.[12] Carling explained this conclusion, based on some previous studies, on four points: First, smugglers have developed new boats purpose-built for smuggling, rather than relying on fishing boats. Second, in order to increase their profit, smugglers double the number of passengers on each journey through the use of larger *pateras* and rubber boats (zodiacs). Third, they organize collective journeys to include a group of *pateras* which spread out when they approach the coast. This makes it difficult for the Guardia Civil to intercept all the boats that have been detected by the SIVE. Fourth, the SIVE program makes the journey of immigrants, especially those who lack nautical skills, more dangerous, while the smugglers run no additional risk of arrest by Spanish authorities.[13] Additionally, in reaction to sophisticated virtual-control systems applied in the western Mediterranean and in the Atlantic Ocean, immigrants try to reach European soil from eastern Maghrebi coasts (from Algeria, Tunisia, and Libya) especially via the Italian islands of Lampedusa, Pantelleria, Linosa and mainland Sicily. Moreover, it must be stressed that irregular immigrants who enter Spain, as well as other host countries, by sea are heavily outweighed by immigrants entering via other channels.

This chapter, first, demonstrates controversial aspects of the Ceuta and Melilla fences as a southern border of the EU. Second, it highlights the changing roles of the two enclaves' fences.

Fences of Ceuta and Melilla: A Controversial EU Border

Fencing the borders of Ceuta and Melilla has stimulated many complicated and unresolved questions between Spain and Morocco. The seriousness of these questions lies in their transitivity and interdependence because they do not stop at the Moroccan-Spanish

---

12 Jørgen Carling, "Migration Control and Migrant Fatalities at the Spanish-African Borders", p. 327.

13 *Ibid.*, p. 327.

border, but rather they extend beyond bilateral relations between the two countries.

A Fault Line between Two Different Spheres

The fences of Ceuta and Melilla are not just a land border between two neighboring countries, but they are built upon "a complex amalgamation of clashes and alliances"[14] representing a "multi-faceted fault line" between Spain and Morocco. The two countries represent an ex-colonizer and an ex-colonized, respectively, two peoples (Spaniards and Moroccans), two nations (Westerns and Arabs), two religions (Christianity and Islam), two continents (Europe and Africa), and two regions (Western Europe and Arab Maghreb). Indeed, the fences around the two enclaves, as the first European walls that were built after the destruction of the Berlin wall, are "a stark and literal reminder of the cultural, political and economic barriers that remain to be overcome between Europe and its Mediterranean neighbors".[15] However, these frontiers are not necessarily similar to Huntington's fault lines[16] of war and conflict. On the contrary, the Mediterranean has been for a long time a sphere of coexistence and interaction.

Concerning the cultural aspect of this border between Spain and Morocco, it is noteworthy that the beginning of the twenty-first century has witnessed an increase in cultural misunderstandings, especially between the Muslim and Western worlds. There are many factors that contribute to the current cultural tensions between the two worlds: immigration, terrorism, foreign policy of some western countries toward the Muslim World (Iraq, Palestine, Afghanistan…), the meaning of freedom of speech and media especially in the West (e.g., the cartoon crisis), restraints and restrictions on the religious freedom in the two

---

14   Xavier Ferrer-Gallardo, "The Spanish-Moroccan Border Complex: Processes of Geopolitical, Functional and Symbolic Rebordering", *Political Geography*, Vol. 27, No. 3 (2008), p. 303.

15   Peter Gold, *Europe or Africa?: A Contemporary Study of the Spanish North African Enclaves of Ceuta and Melilla*. Liverpool: Liverpool University press, 2000, p. 144.

16   Samuel Huntington argued in his famous book *The Clash of Civilizations and the Remaking of World Order* (New York: Simon and Schuster, 1996) that the modern conflicts take place between two or more identity groups (usually religious or ethnic) from different civilizations. He alleged civilizational fault lines replaced the political and ideological boundaries of the Cold War.

worlds (e.g., the prohibition and obstruction of the exercise of some religious rites and aspects like the headscarf). These misunderstandings have become sometimes crucial and critical, reflecting the vulnerability of the relationship between the two worlds.

In fact, some scholars, politicians and activists in the two nations focus on these tensions to show only one side of the coin. For example, Samuel Huntington's thesis of the "Clash of Civilizations" argued that that cultural factors are and would continue to be the fundamental source of current and future conflicts. According to Huntington, "differences among civilizations are not only real, they are basic. Civilizations are differentiated from each other by history, language, culture, tradition and most importantly, religion".[17] Huntington concluded pessimistically that "the Clash of Civilizations will dominate global politics. The fault lines between civilizations will be the battle lines of the future".[18] According to José Maria Aznar, the former Spanish Prime Minister, the clash between the two nations began in the eighth century. Aznar said, in a lecture delivered at Georgetown University on 21 September 2004, that Spain's long battle against terrorism started as early as 711, when Muslims, led by Tariq Ibn Ziyad, invaded Spain. He further argued that the terrorist acts which struck Madrid on 11 March 2004, did not begin with the Iraqi crisis but with the fall of al-Andalus.[19] Such an arbitrary and biased version of history ignores the greatest part of peaceful and cooperative relations that had been in the region for more than 12 centuries.

Despite the long Spanish occupation of Ceuta and Melilla, the Spanish position regarding the two enclaves is still marked by doubt and suspicion. It anticipates a potential Islamic threat that will come either from inside of the two towns — reflecting the expressions of rejection of the occupation voiced by the Muslim population — or from Morocco, which has neither officially nor popularly recognized the Spanishness of the enclaves.

---

17 Samuel Huntington, "The Clash of Civilizations", *Foreign Affairs*, Vol. 72, No. 3 (1993), p. 25.

18 *Ibid.*

19 Mohamed Larbi Messari, "The Vivid Memories of Al-Andalus in the Discourse on Dialogue among Civilisations", http://www.isesco.org.ma/english/publications/Human%20Civilizations/p32.php

The demographics of the two cities has not carried significance until the beginning of twenty-first century. While the number of Muslims is increasing faster than other groups, the Spanish community is gradually decreasing because of relocation to the peninsula and a low birth rate. This shifting population explains some of the anxiety Spanish authors express about the growth of the number of Muslims not only in Ceuta and Melilla but in the whole of Spain. For instance, Herrero de Miñón, who is one of the fathers of the Spanish Constitution,[20] argued in favor of immigration policies that filter applicants for their "linguistic and cultural affinity", with the underlying purpose of excluding Moroccans and favoring Latin-Americans, Romanians and Slavs. The point seems to be that these immigrants do not threaten the notion of Spanishness as much as Moroccanization does.[21]

Despite this pessimistic view, most people all over the world remain optimistic about the relationships between civilizations and cultures, emphasizing the common denominators of nations that would enhance mutual understanding and trust. The thesis of "Dialogue among Civilizations", as the alternative paradigm, has been proposed by a large number of the world's intelligentsia. It states that the diversity of the world's cultures and religions are natural and inherent and that they are elements that contribute to the wealth of our planet.[22]

The two enclaves have always been open to other Moroccan neighboring cities and areas. Many people of Northern Morocco speak Spanish fluently because of the different kinds of contact with Spaniards. Some of them can be considered as "frontier workers": they work in the enclaves, especially in commerce and construction, but retain their habitual residence in adjacent Moroccan provinces to which they normally return every day or at least once a week. So, the fences enclose Ceuta and Melilla and increase their isolation from neighboring inhabitants.

There are many factors that suggest Moroccan-Spanish cultural relations are flourishing. Common historical heritage, geographical

---

20 Miguel Herrero y Rodriguez de Miñón is considered to be one of the seven fathers of the Spanish Constitution (1978).
21 Jaume Castan Pinos, "Identity Challenges affecting the Spanish Enclaves of Ceuta and Melilla", *Nordlit*, No. 24 (2009), pp. 76–77.
22 Said Saddiki, "El Papel de la Diplomacia Cultural en las Relaciones Internacionales", *Revista CIDOB d'Afers Internacionales*, No. 88 (December 2009), p. 115.

proximity and social and economic interactions are important factors for the promotion of cultural relations between the two countries. Disregarding long-lasting disputes, including the current situation and the future of the two enclaves, Spain has been for some time the second most important economic partner of Morocco, after France.

Ceuta and Melilla: An Unresolved Issue

The dispute between Morocco and Spain over Spanish-controlled territories in North Africa began at the sunset of the fifteenth century and the beginning of sixteenth century when Spain and Portugal occupied some Moroccan ports. Although Melilla has been under Spanish sovereignty since 1497 and Ceuta since 1668, Moroccans have never recognized Spanish sovereignty over these enclaves and other rocky islands, and always considered them as integral parts of Moroccan territory.

Since obtaining its independence in 1956, Morocco has never ceased to call for the restoration of all Spanish-controlled territories in Northern Morocco. In its first document submitted to the United Nations as a member of this organization, Morocco provided a list of unresolved territorial disputes with Spain, including the two enclaves. The Moroccan government has taken every occasion to reiterate their position. On 27 January 1975, the Permanent Mission of Morocco to the UN submitted a memorandum (A/AC-109–475) to the Special Committee on Decolonization requesting that all territories controlled by Spain in Northern Morocco be placed on the UN list of non-self-governing territories.

Morocco bases its request for recovering Spanish-controlled territories in Northern Morocco on historical, geographical, juridical and geopolitical grounds. With regard to historical reasons, Morocco is one of the existing oldest monarchies in the world, and it had ruled without dispute its coasts and ports located at Western North Africa, including Ceuta and Melilla. Before the coming of the Europeans, Ceuta and Melilla had never been *terra nullius* ("no-man's land"); rather, they were two important Islamic cities in North Africa since the arrival of Islam to the region. For example, in the fifteenth century, Ceuta had over a thousand mosques, 62 libraries, 43 educational institutions and

1 university.[23] With the Arrival of Moulay Idriss I in Morocco and the establishment of the first Islamic state in Western North Africa in 788, all Moroccan dynasties have exercised sovereignty over the enclaves and all Moroccan Mediterranean coasts.

Morocco also justifies its demands by invoking the principle of territorial integrity and decolonization laid down in the Charter of the UN. It is worth mentioning that Morocco underwent colonialism under multiple countries during the period of European colonial expansion, and it had been divided into several colonies; for that reason, Moroccans consider the existence of Spain in North African as a "museum of colonialism".

Morocco linked the future of Ceuta and Melilla to that of Gibraltar for a certain period of the 1960s and 1970s. This approach was known in Morocco as "Hassan II's doctrine", which means that the resolution of the issue of Spanish-controlled areas in Northern Morocco should not be dissociated from the settlement of the Gibraltar question.[24]The Spanish government indicated to King Hassan II in the 1960s that there was a prospect of ceding the two enclaves to Morocco once Gibraltar was returned to Spain.[25] Hassan II declared on 25 November 1975, that "sometime in the future, England will logically restore Gibraltar to Spain. If the English restore Gibraltar to Spain, the later should restore Ceuta and Melilla to us".[26] However, in the mid-1980s, Morocco decided to separate the future of Ceuta and Melilla from the question of Gibraltar. In 1987, King Hassan II stated, "My attitude towards Ceuta and Melilla is that this is a question of an anachronistic situation which cannot be compared to that of Gibraltar, given that Gibraltar is in Europe.

23   R. Rezette, *The Spanish Enclaves in Morocco*. Paris: Nouvelles Editions Latines, 1976, p. 27. Cited in Gerry O'Reilly, *Ceuta and the Spanish Sovereign Territories: Spanish and Moroccan Claims*. Durham: International Boundaries Research Unit [Dept. of Geography, University of Durham], 1994, p. 2.

24   Mohamed Larbi Messari, "The Current Context of a Moroccan Claim to Ceuta and Melilla", *Dafatir Siyassiya*, No. 107 (December 2009) [in Arabic].

25   Robert Swann, "Gibraltar: The Cheerful Mongrel", *New Society*, Vol. 5, No. 127 (4 March 1965), p. 7. Cited by Robert Aldrich and John Connell, *The Last Colonies*. Cambridge: Cambridge University Press, 1998, p. 226.

26   *Maroc-Soir* (26 November 1975), cited by Raobert Rézette, *The Spanish Enclaves in Morocco*. Paris: Nouvelles Editions Latines, 1976, p. 146.

Gibraltar is under the control of a European power, allied through the EC and NATO to Spain".[27]

Morocco does not leave any opportunity to communicate its position on the two enclaves and small islands to its interlocutors. This position was included in Morocco's memorandum to the EC when they signed the cooperation agreement by stating that this agreement did not mean recognition of the situation of Ceuta and Melilla (memorandum of 28 May 1988). Before that time, the Diplomatic Representation of Morocco to the European Communities informed the Secretariat-General of the European Commission a similar memorandum regarding the status of the enclaves on the occasion of Spain's accession to the EU.

One of the strongest incidents regarding this issue of a UN framework came on 7 September 1988 when Abdellatif Filali, Moroccan Foreign Minister at that time, addressed the General Assembly in New York. He placed his remarks in the context of the importance of stability and security in the Mediterranean and good relations with the European Community, stating that "it is imperative to resolve the dispute concerning the enclaves of Ceuta and Melilla and other small Mediterranean islands under Spanish occupation, in order to prevent this anachronistic situation — a consequence of earlier times — from threatening the essential harmony which should prevail over the relations between the two countries situated on either sides of the Strait of Gibraltar".[28]

King Hassan II proposed in January 1987 that a committee of experts be set up to discuss the future of Ceuta and Melilla, but, unfortunately, Spain's government did not officially respond and continually refused to enter into any negotiation with Morocco about the two towns. On 3 March 1994, on the 33rd anniversary of Throne Day, Hassan II called once again for the establishment of a committee of experts, and he reaffirmed Morocco's inalienable rights to the enclaves. In September 1997, the former Moroccan Prime Minister, Abdellatif Filali, in his speech before the UN General Assembly, underscored the position, referring

27   Robert Aldrich and John Connell, *The Last Colonies*, p. 226.
28   *El Pais* (October 8, 1988) cited in Peter Gold, *Europe or Africa?: A Contemporary Study of the Spanish North African Enclaves of Ceuta and Melilla*, p. 13

to the enclaves as "Moroccan towns under Spanish occupation" and calling for a solution following the example of Hong Kong and Macau.[29]

For his part, King Mohammed VI did not hesitate in a speech on 30 July 2002 to reaffirm explicitly the necessity to enter into dialogue with Spain about this critical issue. He also renewed his father's proposal to establish a Moroccan-Spanish joint committee for finding a solution to the problem of all areas controlled by Spain in Northern Morocco.

On 6 November 2007, a visit to Ceuta and Melilla by the King of Spain, Juan Carlos, threatened relations between Morocco and Spain. Morocco strongly condemned this visit, which was viewed by King Mohammed VI as having "counter-productive" effects that could "put in danger" future relations between the two countries. He said that it showed the Spanish government's "flagrant lack of respect for the mission and spirit of the 1991 Treaty of Friendship and Cooperation" between the two neighbouring countries.[30]

Europeanization of Ceuta and Melilla Fences: A Paradox of EU Foreign Policy

On the basis of the Schengen Agreement, the EU "External Border" refers to the frontiers between member and non-member states. But some analysts state that, according to new European policies concerning the externalization of EU Migration Management, common EU borders can no longer be considered simply as a geographical issue. Rather, they are "located where the management strategy begins".[31] In this sense, in recent years, "Africa's sub-Saharan countries have become EU's southern border".[32] In a strict territorial sense, however, the Ceuta and Melilla fences represent the *de facto* southern frontier of EU.

---

29 *Ibid.*, p. 25.
30 See the summary of King Mohammed VI's statement on this event, "S.M. le Roi rend publique sa position sur la visite de Juan Carlos aux villes occupées Sebta et Melillia", *Le Matin*, 6 November 2007, http://lematin.ma/journal/2006/Presidant-hier-a-Casablanca-un-Conseil-des-ministres_S-M--le-Roi-rend-publique-sa-position-sur-la-visite-de-Juan-Carlos-aux-villes-occupees-Sebta-et-Melillia/1516.html
31 Pablo Ceriani *et al.*, "Report on the Situation on the Euro-Mediterranean Borders", Work package 9 [University of Barcelona] (27 April 2009), p. 2.
32 *Ibid.*, p. 3.

Since the adoption of the Schengen Agreement in 1985 which allowed the free movement of EU citizens within member states, the control of external European Community borders was no longer a matter for each European state to resolve independently but a common European problem. Therefore, after joining the European Community in 1986, Spain was compelled, according to its European commitments, to tighten its border control measures.

As the Spanish government initiated its Action Plan for sub-Saharan Africa (2005–2008) — known also as the "Africa Plan" — to control immigration influxes, the Europeanization of its immigration policies became a key element of its agenda.

Preventing irregular immigration, which remains the principal stated purpose for the fences of Ceuta and Melilla, led ultimately to the involvement of the EU in financing this project. Spain is always backed politically and financially by the EU in its policy concerning the imposition of a *status quo* in North Africa as a part of its "Fortress Europe" strategy. During the 1990s, the EU pressed Spain to control its borders; nowadays it is Spain that is increasingly urging the EU to consider border control as a European issue[33] in order to get more financial and political support. For example, the cost of the first fencing project around Ceuta (1995–2000) totaled EUR 48 million, 75 percent of which was financed by the EU.[34] Undoubtedly, financing the fences of the two enclaves is the key aspect of Europeanization of this question.

One of the major criticisms of this EU global approach to immigration is that the management of trans-Mediterranean migration does not need unilateral initiatives drawn up by EU and its members, regardless of their effectiveness. Instead, it requires a comprehensive solution that takes into account the human rights of immigrants, the complexity of irregular trans-national migration and the interests and conception of transit countries such as Morocco.

On the other hand, the building of fences around the enclaves takes place in a paradoxical context. Today, the Mediterranean sphere is being pulled in two different directions: one toward more complementarity

---

33 Ricard Zapata-Barrero and Nynke De witte, "The Spanish Governance of EU Borders: Normative Questions", *Mediterranean Politics*, Vol. 12, No. 1 (2007), p. 89.
34 Stefan Alscher, "Knocking at the Doors of 'Fortress Europe': Immigration and Border Control in Southern Spain and Eastern Poland", p. 11.

and integration and the other toward the delineation tangible and intangible boundaries. Concerning the first direction, the Mediterranean basin has been for centuries a space of coexistence between the people on both sides, acting as a bridge between them regardless their ethnic, cultural and religious traditions. On the basis of this vision, EU and its Mediterranean partners have begun, since the collapse of the Berlin wall in 1989, thinking and talking about many important projects of cooperation and partnership between the countries of the two shores. This process culminated with the Conference of Barcelona in 1995 that brought together EU member states and 10 Mediterranean partners (Algeria, Egypt, Israel, Jordan, Lebanon, Morocco, the Palestinian Authority, Syria, Tunisia and Turkey).

In the Barcelona Declaration, the Euro-Mediterranean partners established the three main objectives of the Partnership:

1. Political and Security Objectives: Definition of a common area of peace and stability through the reinforcement of political and security dialogue.

2. Economic and Financial Objectives: Construction of a zone of shared prosperity through an economic and financial partnership and the gradual establishment of a free-trade area.

3. Social, Cultural and Human Objectives: Rapprochement between peoples through a social, cultural and human partnership aimed at encouraging understanding between cultures and exchanges between civil societies.

More than a decade after the Barcelona Declaration, then-French President Nicolas Sarkozy launched the Union for the Mediterranean initiative which was approved by an international conference that took place in Paris on 13 July 13 2008. Leaders from the 27 EU nations and their 16 Middle East and North Africa partners participated. Although the Union for the Mediterranean intends, according to its founders, to reinforce the Euro-Mediterranean Partnership, it is seen by many commentators as the failure of the Barcelona Process.

With regard to the relationship between Morocco and the EU, Morocco is always considered by Europeans as an important ally, a credible interlocutor and an effective intermediary between Arab and Western Worlds. Recognizing political and judicial reforms made by

Morocco in recent years, the EU granted it an "advanced status" in October 2008. Morocco is the first country in the southern Mediterranean region to benefit from such "advanced status" in its relations with the EU. It raises the status of Morocco to something more than a partner but less than a member, and as Taieb Fassi Fihri, former Moroccan Foreign Minister, quoting the words of Romano Prodi,[35] put it "the new status gives Morocco everything except the institutions".

The question may be asked: to what extent could the Mediterranean countries reconcile their national interest in classical notion of sovereignty and realpolitik theory with the external pressures imposed both by a "globalizing" world and the significant development in international human rights law (especially international law pertaining to migrant workers and refugees)? Concerning the subject of this chapter, another challenge arises from the disputed sovereignty over Spanish-controlled territories in Northern Morocco. The enclaves of Ceuta and Melilla may be for Morocco, just as Gibraltar is for Spain, an ongoing "stone in one's shoe".[36] Without resolving the situation of these territories peacefully and bilaterally, it will be difficult to expect a complete success of cooperative projects taking place in the region. Rather, it will be always a hindrance to achieving a stable and long-term partnership, mainly between Spain and Morocco.

Changing Roles of Ceuta and Melilla Fences

Although the Spanish government has constantly stated that fences of the two enclaves aim only to stop irregular immigration, a comprehensive view of various aspects of the issue leads us to surmise the existence of other objectives behind this policy. Moreover, the stated and hidden objectives of this policy are not fixed but, rather, change according to regional circumstances, national interests, the balance of power and the nature of relations between Morocco and Spain.

---

35 The former President of the European Commission.
36 The description of the enclaves as a "stone in shoe" is used by Peter Gold in his book entitled: *A Stone in Spain's Shoe: The Search for the Solution for the Problem of Gibraltar*. Liverpool: Liverpool University Press, 1994. See also Evgeny Vinokurov, *A Theory of Enclaves*. Lanham, MD: Lexington Books, 2007, p. 3.

Preventing Irregular Immigration:
Towards "Fortress Europe"

The fences of the two enclaves can be considered as an externalization of the problem of irregular migration. EU member states have initiated several projects and initiatives in the last two decades[37] that are aimed at exporting internal migration and asylum problems to neighboring countries and, in particular, to countries geographically closest in order to relieve the burden of undesired immigration in Europe.[38]

Contrary to the integration process and "open door" policy led by the Euro-Mediterranean partners in the last two decades, there is an exclusive process by which EU member states practice a strict policy of "closing the door" towards the movement of people from non-European countries. Saskia Sassen eloquently describes this paradox:

> Economic globalization denationalizes national economies; in contrast, immigration is renationalizing politics. There is a growing consensus in the community of states to lift border controls for the flow of capital, information, and services, and more broadly, to further globalization. But when it comes to immigrants and refugees, whether in North America, Western Europe, or Japan, the national state claims all its old splendor in asserting its sovereign right to control its borders. On this matter, there is also a consensus in the community of states.[39]

The recent forms of transnational immigration and their consequences are seen by many observers as a sign of erosion of the fundamental elements of the nation-state. Moreover, all governments, especially in Europe and North America, believe that this transnational immigration is a direct threat to national sovereignty and socio-economic stability. Thus, they have been attempting not simply to control or organize

---

37 The so-called "external dimension" of EU immigration and asylum policy was not formally embraced by the European Council until October 1999. See Christian Boswell, "The 'External Dimension' of EU Immigration and Asylum Policy", *International Affairs*, Vol. 79, No. 3 (2003), p. 620.

38 Ounia Doukouré and Helen Oger, "The EC External Migration Policy: The Case of the MENA Countries", research paper 2007/06, European University Institute, *RSCAS* (2007), p. 3, http://cadmus.eui.eu/bitstream/handle/1814/7991/CARIM-RR_2007_06.pdf

39 Saskia Sassen, *Losing Control? Sovereignty in an Age of Globalization*. New York: Columbia University Press, 1996, p. 63.

immigration flows but instead to stop them by passing strict immigration laws and building border walls and fences.

Despite all efforts made by governments to control trans-national flows, the number of people crossing international borders every day by regular or irregular channels, with the intention to stay temporarily or permanently outside their home land, has been rising gradually.[40]

Today, more people live outside their country of origin than at any time in history. According to the UN Population Division 244 million were living outside their country of origin in 2015, up from 222 million in 2010 and 173 million in 2000. Nearly two thirds of all international migrants live in Europe (76 million) or Asia (75 million). North America hosted the third largest number of international migrants (54 million), followed by Africa (21 million), Latin America and the Caribbean (9 million) and Oceania (8 million).[41]

Spain is the seventh largest host country in the world with 6.9 million immigrants. It was also ranked seventh among countries in the world with the highest remittance-sending rates, with USD 12.6 billion being sent in 2010. An important proportion of these remittances were transferred to Morocco, as the eighteenth-highest receiver of remittances of the world's countries. In the same period, Morocco received USD 6.4 billion from its expatriates all over the world.[42] With respect to international irregular immigrants, it is impossible to obtain accurate data about them because of their clandestine and irregular situation. The International Labour Organization estimates, however, that there are roughly 20 to 30 million unauthorized migrants worldwide, comprising around 10 to

---

40 The Department of Economic and Social Affairs of the United Nations affirmed in its International *Migration Report 2015* that "The number of international migrants worldwide has continued to grow rapidly over the past fifteen years reaching 244 million in 2015, up from 222 million in 2010 and 173 million in 2000". The Department of Economic and Social Affairs of the United Nations, *International Migration Report 2015: Highlights* (New York: United Nations, 2016), p. 1, http://www.un.org/en/development/desa/population/migration/publications/migrationreport/docs/MigrationReport2015_Highlights.pdf

41 *Ibid.*

42 *Migration and Remittances Factbook 2011—2nd edition.* Washington: The World Bank, 2010, pp. 1–15, https://openknowledge.worldbank.org/bitstream/handle/10986/23743/9781464803192.pdf

15 percent of the world's immigrants.[43] Each year, an estimated 2.5 to 4 million immigrants cross international borders without authorization.[44]

Since western European countries adopted strict immigration policies, Morocco and Spanish-controlled enclaves in North Africa have turned into important points of departure of irregular immigration flows into European countries on the northern shore of the Mediterranean, namely Spain, Italy and France. Needless to say, the fences of Ceuta and Melilla were built to prevent Sub-Saharan African immigrants, not Moroccans, for two reasons. First, according to the Agreement on the Accession of Spain to the EU, inhabitants of Tetouan and Nador, two Moroccan provinces adjacent to Ceuta and Melilla, became exempted from visa requirements and enabled Moroccans to cross the enclave's border but not to enter mainland Spain. Secondly, Moroccans from outside these two provinces can be expelled if they overstay their visa period or enter the enclaves illegally under the Agreement of Return signed between Morocco and Spain in 1992.

Sub-Saharan African immigrants who intend to use Morocco simply as a transit route may find that the "transit country" becomes a "host country" if they face difficulties entering Europe, whether by sea or through Ceuta and Melilla. For some time, a large number of immigrants failing or not venturing to enter Europe have built temporary settlements as a "third nation" or a "waiting room" on Moroccan territory near Ceuta and Melilla; it is a place where seekers live who cannot reach their Eldorado nor can they return to their home countries.

Since 2005, thousands of sub-Saharan-African migrants have tried to climb over the fences of Ceuta and Melilla using makeshift ladders. Some of them died in these tragic attempts to reach the two enclaves. These events have deeply shocked the public and require a collective, trans-national approach to tackle. Although these events implicated transit countries, especially Maghreb countries, the EU and Spain continue to give preference to unilateral and security initiatives based on the militarization of EU territorial and maritime borders despite

---

43 International Labour Office, Towards a Fair Deal for Migrant Workers in the Global Economy [International Labour Conference, 92nd Session]. Geneva: International Labour Office, 2004.

44 The Global Commission on International Immigration, "Immigration in an Interconnected World: New Directions for Action" (October 2005), p. 85.

repeated demonstrations of their inability to cope with trans-national flows of irregular immigrants. Its "calculated" involvement of the transit countries as one of the forms of the externalization of borders control suggests that the EU intends to make them gendarmes or buffer zones.

Morocco as a transit country, finds itself in a crucial situation between a rock and a hard place. For the last two decades it has been under EU pressure to control its territorial boundaries and stop the flows of sub-Saharan immigrants who intend to enter to Europe through Moroccan coasts or the Ceuta and Melilla enclaves. On the other hand, Morocco faces a growing demand from national and international human-rights groups to provide more protection to irregular immigrants crossing or settling on its territory.

Spanish efforts to build and strengthen fences around Ceuta and Melilla have faced great opposition not only from Morocco, since it does not recognize Spanish sovereignty over these enclaves, but also from some European diplomats and human-rights organizations. The significant development in this context is the increasing awareness among some European statesmen of the ineffectiveness of such separation fences. According to one European diplomat,

> Illegal immigration is a growing problem, but we can't just build a wall around the EU. We need to encourage economic development in other countries, through both trade and aid, so that people have better opportunities in their own countries. At the same time, we have to balance firm but fair immigration policies with a compassionate attitude to refugees and asylum seekers. It's a fine line to walk.[45]

The former European Commissioner for Justice, Freedom and Security, Franco Frattini, said "Europe cannot become a fortress" and "must do all it can to avoid sending this kind of negative message to other countries. [...] measures like building higher and higher fences will not resolve the problem of unwanted immigration.[46]

---

45   *Christian Science Monitor*, August 1998. Cited in Shelagh Furness, "Brave new Borderless State: Illegal Immigration and the External Borders of the EU", *IBRU Boundary and Security Bulletin* (Autumn 2000), p. 100.
46   Tito Drago, "Spain: From the Berlin Wall to Ceuta and Melilla", *Inter Press Service* (October 5, 2005), http://www.ipsnews.net/2005/10/spain-from -the-berlin-wall-to-ceuta-and-melilla/

The central question in this context is whether the new measures adopted by the Spanish government can prevent desperately poor people from sub-Saharan Africa from attempting to enter Europe through Ceuta and Melilla or through another route, whatever the cost may be, even at the risk of their lives. Today, there is unanimity among researchers that the only effective solution to irregular immigration is to reduce economic crises in developing and underdeveloped countries; to support and encourage political reforms in origin countries, especially in Africa; and to stop all social disturbances and civil wars that have been the main causes of both regular and irregular migration.

To sum up, the militarization of Ceuta and Melilla borders and the building of new fences in an attempt to stop or at least reduce the number of irregular immigrants remain an impractical solution. Such obstructions would simply lead them to cross elsewhere and to find new migratory routes to Spain by boats through the Canary Islands, for example, from Mauritania or Senegal. Trying to stop this kind of migration is like trying to catch water in one's hands; the more you press on the water the more it slips through your fingers. Furthermore, irregular immigrants who reach Spain from Ceuta and Melilla are a minority of all immigrants living in Spain irregularly, and the majority of these entered legally by ports or airports but have overstayed their visas.

A Relative Geopolitical Importance

The geopolitical dimensions of a Spanish presence in North Africa are very significant not only for Spain but also for the EU. Since the entrance of Spain into the EU, the enclaves' fences in Northern Morocco became the EU's only borders with an Arab nation. Moreover, Spain is the only Mediterranean country that could control the two shores of the Mediterranean, because of its presence in North Africa. The EU is aware of this unique and strategic position as both an intercontinental bridge between Europe and Africa and as a lighthouse to control the whole western Mediterranean Sea. This explains why EU members support or at least remain silent toward the Spanish occupation of these territories.

This geopolitical importance is less significant to NATO because, when Spain joined the organization in 1981, the enclaves were explicitly assigned outside the alliance defensive area. NATO members, particularly the U.S., were not willing to defend territories in North Africa as such behaviour risked escalation into a wider conflict in the Middle East.[47] Furthermore, the involvement of NATO in the issue of the two enclaves does not make sense, at least in the medium term, because of Morocco's strong ties with influential countries in the NATO alliance, namely France and the U.S. Moreover, the cooperation of Morocco is crucial for NATO projects in the region. This can be explained, for example, by the meeting of the North Atlantic Council being held in Rabat on 7 April 2006 and by Morocco's contribution to "Operation Active Endeavour".[48]

It is argued that international straits do not concern only their coastal states but are vital for the whole of the international community. So, it is difficult to imagine that any state in the world would accept that one country can control the two shores of the Strait of Gibraltar. This will happen when Spain restores the Rock of Gibraltar, without giving up the Spanish-controlled territories in North Africa to Morocco. The words of Jaime De Pinies, a long-time Spanish diplomat who served as president of the UN General Assembly from 1985–1986, spoken in 1990, are still valuable today: "On the day we can restore the sovereignty of Gibraltar to Spain, it would be hard to imagine that the international community will accept that we control the two shores of the Straits".[49] This notion has often been stressed by Morocco. In this context, King Hassan II argued that "the day Spain comes into possession of Gibraltar, Morocco will, of necessity, get Ceuta and Melilla. No power can permit Spain to possess both keys to the same straits".[50]

---

47   Gerry O'Reilly, *Ceuta and the Spanish Sovereign Territories*: *Spanish and Moroccan Claims*. Durham: International Boundaries Research Unit [Dept. of Geography, University of Durham], 1994, p. 19.

48   Morocco and NATO signed in 22 October 2009 in Naples (Italy) a Tactical Memorandum of Understanding (TMOU) for a Moroccan contribution to NATO's anti-terrorism mission (Operation Active Endeavour).

49   Jaime De Pinies, *La descolonización del Sáhara*: *Un Tema sin Concluir*. Madrid: Espasa Crónica, 1990, p. 55. Cited in Mohamed Larbi Messari, "The Current Context of a Moroccan Claim to Ceuta and Melilla" (December 2009).

50   *L'Opinion* (26 novembre 1975), cited by Robert Rézette, *The Spanish Enclaves in Morocco*. Paris: Nouvelles Editions Latines, 1976, p. 146.

Perpetuating the Current *status quo*: The Long-Term Goal

Spain's policy of building new fences and reinforcing its existing ones occurred in the context of a latent conflict with Morocco over Spanish-controlled territories in North Africa. Fencing the two enclaves is part of a comprehensive strategy which has taken several forms and steps aimed at perpetuating the *status quo*. Granting autonomous status, passing immigration laws and organizing visits by the Spanish King and ministers are key elements of this strategy.

The granting of autonomous status to Ceuta and Melilla, enacted by law on 13 March 1995, was a turning point in the modern history of the two enclaves. Since the adoption of this law, Ceuta and Melilla officially became autonomous cities within the Spanish juridical framework. The granting of autonomy contains a clear message for Morocco to the effect that any claim to recover the enclaves would complicate the *status quo* of Spanish occupation. Moreover, this change-of-status involved the inhabitants of Ceuta and Melilla as third parties in the dispute, which further complicates the question of the two enclaves. Some commentators argue that the loosening of ties between the Spanish central government and the two towns by the granting of autonomy might be regarded as a provocation. By increasing the power of a population, it is even more likely to resist incorporation into Morocco than it was the authorities based in Madrid.[51] This effort coincides with the Spanish government's attempt to change the demographic balance between the two communities living in the enclaves by passing immigration and citizenship laws that impose strict conditions to obtain Spanish citizenship or residence permits.

Legislation, especially immigration and citizenship laws, remains an important instrument by which the Spanish government has tried to maintain the *status quo* of the two enclaves. For example, Spain passed a new immigration law in 1985 in preparation for its entrance into the European Community. According to this law, the majority of Muslims living in the enclaves could only apply for Spanish citizenship after ten

---

51   Robert Aldrich and John Connell, *The Last Colonies*, p. 228.

years of residence. Muslim-born residents in the enclaves were unwilling to apply for the necessary identity card because they did not want to be classified as "foreigners" in the land where they were born. In addition, possession of an identity card meant that they would have to wait ten years to apply for citizenship and there would be no guarantee they would acquire it. On the other hand, without this document, they would be liable for deportation.[52] Fear of the growth of the Muslim population always dominates the Spanish policy and legislation towards the enclaves. It is presumed that such a demographic shift in favor of the Muslim community could alter the current demographic situation and potentially lead to a silent "re-Moroccanization" of the enclaves.

The unprecedented visit of Spain's King Juan Carlos and Queen Sofia to Ceuta and Melilla on 5–6 Novemeber 2007 could be considered as an attempt to "formalize" the current *status quo*. This had been expressed by some right-wing Spanish newspapers. For example, *El Mundo* said in an editorial: "the presence of the King will reaffirm Spanish sovereignty over the two autonomous territories".[53] As an attempt to reject the *de facto* policy applied by the Spanish government in the two enclaves, Morocco denounced this visit and recalled its ambassador to Spain. The danger of theses fences is that the EU financial support for their construction might be considered as an implicit recognition of their being the *de facto* EU southern border.

Conclusion

It is argued in the previous paragraphs that the fences Ceuta and Melilla will continue to influence negatively Morocco's relations with Spain and the EU. Spain's policy to fence the two enclaves' borders reflects contradictory pressures in the region. While the Mediterranean sphere has witnessed an increasing number of cultural and economic cooperation projects in the last two decades, new physical and virtual walls are being built in the region to achieve "Fortress Europe".

---

52 Peter Gold, *Europe or Africa?: A Contemporary Study of the Spanish North African Enclaves of Ceuta and Melilla*, p. 94.
53 "Diplomatic row over King's visit to Ceuta, Melilla", *Expatica*, 2 November 2007, https://www.expatica.com/es/news/Diplomatic-row-over-Kings-visit-to-Ceuta-Melilla_150251.html

The challenge facing the region is whether the growing economic interdependence and bilateral or multilateral institutional mechanisms will prevent any dramatic conflict, or at least a serious crisis, that can cause a major setback to the ongoing Euro-Mediterranean integration process.

Even if North Africa is not currently a priority within international policy agendas, particularly of the U.S., the Strait of Gibraltar will continue to be one of the most vital gateways for commercial and military vessels. Therefore, regardless of the competition for regional influence in the Strait of Gibraltar and any unrest between Morocco and Spain that may be fuelled by the continued Spanish occupation of Ceuta and Melilla, maintaining the current *status quo* in the region remains the most acceptable option for all international actors concerned.

4. The U.S.-Mexico Border Wall[1]

The United States has a long history of immigration. It has attracted immigrants from all over the world since the first European settlers arrived on the American shores, and today has one of the world's highest migration rates. However, it is accurate to say that, from a legal point of view, the Declaration of Independence of 1776 and the Treaty of Paris of 1783, which accorded to the U.S. recognition as a nation, mark the beginning of the country's immigration history. Immigration flows have been a major source of U.S. population growth and have greatly enriched its culture and history. The United States remains home to the largest number of international migrants in the world. Today, according to the U.S. Census Bureau (2010 American Community Survey), there are 36.7 million foreign-born persons legally residing in the U.S., making up 12 percent of the nation's population;[2] more than half (58 percent) do not have American citizenship. Approximately half of them were born in Latin America and almost one-third were born in Mexico.

---

1 Part of this chapter is drawn, with permission from the publisher, from: "Border Fences as an Anti-immigration Device: A Comparative View of American and Spanish Policies", in Elisabeth Vallet (Ed.), *Borders, Fences and Walls: State of Insecurity?* Farnham: Ashgate Publishing, 2014, pp. 175–90.

2 According to the International Organization of Migration, in 2010 immigrants make 13.5 % of the U.S. population; and the net migration rate between 2005 and 2010 was 3.3 migrant(s)/1000 population. *World Migration Report 2010: The Future of Migration: Building Capacities for Change.* Geneva, Switzerland: IOM, 2010, https://publications.iom.int/system/files/pdf/wmr_2010_english.pdf

 https://doi.org/10.11647/OBP.0121.05

Immigration flows to the U.S. are not related to temporary circumstances and have never ceased since the first white man set foot on North American soil. Statistics from recent decades indicate that more than 1.5 million new immigrants settle in the country every year.[3]

In general, there is convergence in the estimates of the number of undocumented migrants in the United States. For example, the Department of Homeland Security estimates that the unauthorized immigrant population living in the country decreased to 10.8 million in January 2009 from 11.6 million in January 2008. Between 2000 and 2009, the unauthorized population grew by 27 percent. Of all unauthorized immigrants living in the United States in 2009, 63 percent entered before 2000, and 62 percent were from Mexico.[4] A report by the Pew Hispanic Center put the estimate at 11.1 million unauthorized immigrants living in the country in March 2009, about a million fewer than in 2007.[5] Approximately 80 percent of them are of Hispanic origin. It should be noted that Mexico as well as being the major country of origin of irregular migration to the U.S. also functions as a transit country for illegal migration from Latin America and a point of entry to the U.S.

In 2013, the United States ranked first in the world as an immigration host country with 46.1 million immigrants, and the Mexico-U.S. border was the largest migration corridor with 13 million users. In the same period, the United States was ranked first as a remittance-sending country, with USD 56 billion being sent abroad. A large part of this remittance was sent to Mexico which ranked, with USD 25.7 billion, as the third largest remittance-receiving country.[6]

---

3   Cf. especially statistics gathered by the U.S. Census Bureau available at https://www.census.gov/

4   Michael Hoefer, Nancy Rytina and Bryan C. Baker, "Estimates of the Unauthorized Immigrant Population Residing in the United States: January 2009", U.S. Department of Homeland Security, Office of Immigration Statistics (January 2010), http://www.dhs.gov/xlibrary/assets/statistics/publications/ois_ill_pe_2009.pdf

5   Jeffrey S. Passel and D'Vera Cohn, "U.S. Unauthorized Immigration Flows are Down Sharply since Mid-Decade", *The Pew Hispanic Center* (1 September 2010), p. i.

6   *Migration and Remittances Factbook 2016*, 3rd edition. Washington: The World Bank Group, 2016, pp. 1–5, https://openknowledge.worldbank.org/bitstream/handle/10986/23743/9781464803192.pdf

From the "Open Border" Policy to Anti-Immigration Legislation

The regulation of immigration in the United States is much older than other western immigrant-receiving countries. The regulation of immigration to the U.S. dates backs to the end of the eighteenth century, specifically to 1798, the year in which three important acts concerning the status of aliens in the United States (the Naturalization Acts, the Alien Friends Act and the Alien Enemies Act) were adopted. Nearly a century later, in 1891, Congress passed the "Immigration Act", which is considered to be the country's first comprehensive immigration law. Subsequently, U.S. lawmakers created a number of acts to regulate the immigration influx and to redefine the status of aliens in the country. One of the most important legislations on the topic, the Immigration and Nationality Act (INA) of 1952, also known as the McCarran-Walter Act, restricted immigration into the United States. According to the U.S. Citizenship and Immigration Services, the INA collected and codified many existing provisions and reorganized the structure of immigration law. The Act has been amended many times over the years, but it still represents the basic body of legislation on immigration, providing the country with a variety of legislative instruments in the field of migration. Until recent decades, however, the American government had not seen immigration as a serious threat and had paid little attention to the issue. For example, the platform of the Republican Party did not even mention immigration control until 1980, and only four years later did it affirm the country's right to control its borders, expressing concern about illegal immigration.[7] This set off a flurry of immigration laws in the late 1980s-2000s aimed at preventing irregular immigrants from entering the country. The Immigration Reform and Control Act (IRCA), adopted by Congress in 1986, increased border enforcement and introduced sanctions for knowingly hiring irregular aliens. This act marks the beginning of a stringent legislative policy. The Illegal Immigration Reform and Immigrant Responsibility Act (IIRIRA)

---

7   Joseph Nevins, "'Illegal Aliens' and the Political Geography of Criminalized Immigrants", paper presented at the annual meeting of the Association of American Geographers [Boston] (8 March1998), cited in Peter Andreas, *Border Games*: *Policing the US-Mexico Divide*. Ithaca, NY and London: Cornell University Press, 2000, p. 86.

released in 1996 placed further restrictions on irregular and irregular immigration by making, for example, access to welfare benefits more difficult for legal aliens and by tightening border control by allocating USD 12 million for a 14-mile triple fence along the U.S.-Mexico border from San Diego eastward.

One of the most important aspects of international immigration currently is the link between immigration and security and criminality in the national policies of host countries. This aspect has been more obvious, especially after 9/11 events, so that illegal immigration has been presented as a possible national-security threat. Mathew Coleman[8] documented two significant recent shifts in U.S. immigration policing in conjunction with the border militarization process. Firstly, since the mid-1990s, lawmakers have sought to bind immigration control to criminal law enforcement so that a criminal conviction can be used as grounds for deportation from the U.S. Coleman argued that this mode of immigration governance means that immigration law is ultimately exempted from judicial review, even as it works largely on the basis of criminal law. Secondly, a concerted effort on the part of lawmakers and the Bush administration, particularly since 9/11, has been made to use local proxy forces — or non-federal delegates — to enforce immigration law. Coleman concluded that, taken together, the criminalization of immigration law and the enrolment of proxy immigration officers at sub-state level constitute a new localized or rescaled geopolitics of immigration policing.[9] In summary, since the 9/11 attacks, several legislative measures have been taken to tighten security control on the U.S. borders with Mexico and Canada. Furthermore, in the immediate aftermath of 9/11, some American politicians called for severe restrictions on immigrant admissions to the United States, and many "anti-illegal" immigration groups have taken advantage of the opportunity to increase their demands.

The U.S. immigration policy entered a new phase after the election of Donald Trump to the U.S. presidency and marked a sharp break with previous policy. The new president has adopted many bills concerning illegal immigrants, deportation, security border control and banning

---

8   Mathew Coleman, "Immigration Geopolitics beyond the Mexico-US Border", *Antipode*, Vol. 39, No. 1 (2007), p. 56.
9   *Ibid.*

entry from seven majority-Muslim countries: Syria, Iraq, Iran, Sudan, Libya, Somalia and Yemen. Trump's Executive Order 13767 on Border Security and Immigration Enforcement Improvements of 25 January 2017 states that irregular immigration presents a clear and present danger to the interests of the United States. This new immigration policy will likely put almost 11 million people who have lived illegally in the U.S. for years or decades at risk of deportation or at least make them live in fear and anxiety.

Regardless of the attractive arguments the Trump administration uses to justify the new immigration legislations, such as the protection of the nation from the foreign terrorists, it will face considerable difficulties in implementing them. For example, the first version of the Trump's Executive Order on Immigration has been temporarily blocked by some federal judges[10] and widely criticized by human-rights advocates and the media.

It is clear that, even if the historical context of immigration regulation in the U.S. is different from other western countries, the objective of its immigration policy is almost the same as all other immigrant-receiving countries. But there is a significant difference in its capacity to absorb new immigrants. The U.S. continues to receive thousands of immigrants from all corners of the world each year, while other western countries — except for the influx of asylum-seekers from the areas of tension, especially Syria — have become fed up with all kinds of new immigrants, especially after the financial crisis of recent years.

Construction of the Border Wall: A Militarization of Immigration Control

The U.S.-Mexico border fences are legitimate under international law since they are built on American territory. Despite critics' claims to the contrary, it is not unlawful for a state to establish fences or walls on its own territory to control access to that territory.

Although the federal government funded the construction of fences around some southern-border cities (Nogales, San Ysidro and El Paso)

---

10   See for example, Mica Rosenberg and Jonathan Stempel, "U.S. Judges Limit Trump Immigration Order; Some Officials Ignore Rulings", *Reuters* (29 January 2017), http://www.reuters.com/article/us-usa-trump-immigration-courts-idUSKBN15D0XG

before the 1990s, it started seriously building fences and escalating control measures along its borders with Mexico in 1994 under Clinton's administration, as a comprehensive policy. The border south of San Diego, which has been identified as an area of high human smuggling and drug trafficking, was the first borderland to be fenced. Republican representative Duncan Hunter, the former Chairman of the House Armed Services Committee, played a significant role in the construction of the first security fence (23 kilometers) on the U.S. southern border separating San Diego County and Tijuana (Mexico).

Fig. 4.1 U.S.-Mexico border fence at Tijuana (6 February 2017).
Photo by Tomas Castelazo, CC BY-SA 4.0.[11]

Since 9/11, irregular immigration has been placed in the same category as terrorism and security threats, including drug trafficking and organized crime. Thus, border-security and a hard-line policy against irregular immigration became key elements of the U.S'.s "war on terror". One of the effects of the 9/11 attacks on the U.S. border-control system was the creation of the Homeland Security Department (HSD). The responsibility for border security transferred from the Department of Justice to the Department of HSD, and Immigration and Naturalization

---

11   Source: Wikimedia Commons, https://commons.wikimedia.org/wiki/File%3A Mexico-US_border_at_Tijuana.jpg

Service was abolished.[12] Shortly after the creation of the Homeland Security Department in 2003, the Border Patrol was directed to formulate a new "National Border Patrol Strategy" that would better reflect the realities of the post 9/11 security landscape. The Border Patrol's strategy comprised five main objectives:

- Establish substantial probability of apprehending terrorists and their weapons as they attempt to enter illegally between the ports of entry;

- Deter illegal entries through improved enforcement;

- Detect, apprehend, and deter smugglers of humans, drugs, and other contraband;

- Leverage "Smart Border" technology to multiply the effect of enforcement personnel; and

- Reduce crime in border communities and consequently improve the quality of life and economic vitality of targeted areas.[13]

On 26 October 2006, then-President George W. Bush signed into law the Secure Fence Act of 2006 (P.L. 109–367), which has been deemed the most important law concerning the reinforcement of the border control. Bush considered the law to be "an important step toward immigration reform" that "will help protect the American people".[14] The Secure Fence Act of 2006 aimed to tighten border security by building 700 miles of double-layered fencing on the U.S.-Mexico border. Further, the law authorized more vehicle barriers, checkpoints and lighting to help prevent people from entering the country illegally. It also authorized the Department of Homeland Security to increase the use of advanced technology like cameras, satellites and unmanned aerial vehicles to reinforce infrastructure at the border. The main goal of the law was to help secure America's borders against irregular entry, drug trafficking and security threats.

---

12   The Homeland Security Act (Public Law 107–296), passed by Congress and signed by the President in November 2002.

13   Department of Homeland Security, Bureau of Customs and Border Protection, "National Border Patrol Strategy" (1 March 2005), p. 2.

14   The White House Archive, "President Bush Signs Secure Fence Act", 26 October 2006, https://georgewbush-whitehouse.archives.gov/news/releases/2006/10/20061026.html

The financial cost of the project has increased year by year. Appropriations for the Homeland Security Department for fiscal year 2007 provided USD 1.2 billion for the installation of fencing, infrastructure and technology along the border; USD 31 million of this total was designated for the completion of the San Diego fence.[15] Appropriations for fencing and other border barriers have increased markedly since the plan entered into force from USD 6 million in fiscal year 2002 to USD 647 million in fiscal year 2007. The fiscal year 2008 appropriation, according to Customs and Border Protection, included USD 196 million for fence construction.[16]

Fig. 4.2 South side of the United States-Mexico border wall in Progreso Lakes, Texas (21 March 2016). Photo by Rebajae, CC BY-SA 3.0.[17]

In general, the construction of border walls and fences leads to diplomatic tensions between neighboring countries because it is

---

15   Chad C. Haddal, Yule Kim and Michael John Garcia, *Border Security: Barriers along the U.S. International Border, RL33659*. Washington, D.C.: Congressional Research Service (16 March 2009), p. 37.

16   *Ibid.*, p. 18.

17   Source: Wikimedia Commons, https://commons.wikimedia.org/wiki/File:United_ States-Mexico-border-wall-Progreso-Lakes-Texas.jpeg

usually viewed as an unfriendly action by targeted countries. The construction of the fence along the U.S.-Mexico border elicited much controversy from internal and external parties. Immediately prior to the 9/11 attacks, the U.S. and Mexico were on the verge of a historic opportunity to rewrite immigration laws and fundamentally alter the migratory relationship between the two nations, regularizing the status of millions of undocumented immigrant workers living in the United States. At that promising moment, the unexpected events of September 11th occurred, which caused relations between the two countries to deteriorate as greater attention, especially from the American side, was paid to national-security concerns and regional perspectives.[18] Mexico opposed the U.S. plan to build more separation fences along the border between the two countries, considering them to be in opposition to the regional integration process in the NAFTA region. Felipe Calderón, then-President of Mexico, stated that

> it is deplorable to go ahead with this decision of the wall at the border [...]. The wall will not solve any problem. Humanity made a huge mistake by building the Berlin Wall and I believe that today the United States is committing a grave error in building the wall on our border. It is much more useful to solve common problems and foster prosperity in both countries.[19]

Although the events of 9/11 were neither connected to Mexican nationals nor committed by attackers entering American territory illegally from Mexico, their long-term effects on U.S.-Mexican migration relations and the regional integration process will last for decades.

Tension between the two neighboring countries has recently escalated because of successive statements by Donald Trump — especially during his 2016 election campaign — who promised to build a border wall.[20] The main point of tension is Trump's call for Mexico to fund the

---

18   Michele Waslin, "The New Meaning of the Border: U.S.-Mexico Migration Since 9/11", paper prepared for the conference on "Reforming the Administration of Justice in Mexico", The Center for U.S.-Mexican Studies, University of California [San Diego] (15–17 May 2003), pp. 10–12, http://escholarship.org/uc/item/3dd8w0r6

19   Ken Herman, "Bush: Border Fence not Enough", *Austin American-Statesman*, 27 October 2006, https://www.pressreader.com/usa/austin-american-states man/20061027/281573761191370

20   It is not actually about a new wall. Rather, Trump's policy aims at extending the barriers that already exist on many parts of the border.

construction of this wall. Immediately after his inauguration, Donald Trump adopted the Executive Order 13767 that aimed at securing the southern border of the U.S. "through the immediate construction of a physical wall on the southern border".[21]

It is estimated that the new wall will cost a great deal of money. According to Mitch McConnell, a Republican congressman, the wall is expected to cost between USD 12–15 billion. Additionally, the maintenance of the wall could cost as much as USD 750 million per year.[22] Moreover, Trump's project will likely face significant funding challenges and practical difficulties, especially in native American reservations.[23] It will have serious environmental effects along the Rio Grande River where the wall cannot be built in the middle of the valley. An electronic-control system is one possible alternative, but such virtual-security walls have proven to be ineffective in North America and elsewhere.

Virtual Fence: Technology in the Face of "Non-traditional Threats"

To adapt to the information age, governments in developed and developing countries have made great efforts in recent decades to incorporate new information and communication technologies (ICTs) in their security policies. Today, border management and administration of immigration has become a high-tech area, especially in the "Global North".

The U.S. has not only built a physical fence along its southern borders but also adopted a virtual system to control its borderlands. The latter

---

21   The White House, "Executive Order: Border Security and Immigration Enforcement Improvements", 25 January 2017, https://www.whitehouse.gov/the-press-office/2017/01/25/executive-order-border-security-and-immigration-enforcement-improvements

22   Kate Drew, "This is What Trump's Border Wall could Cost", *CNBC* (26 January 2017), http://www.cnbc.com/2015/10/09/this-is-what-trumps-border-wall-could-cost-us.html

23   The U.S. Interior Secretary Ryan Zinke admitted that building the border wall "is complex in some areas". See Matthew Daly and Alicia A. Caldwell, "Zinke: Border Wall 'Complex', Faces Geographic Challenges", *Washington Times* (29 March 2017), http://www.washingtontimes.com/news/2017/mar/29/zinke-border-wall-complex-faces-geographic-challen/

system, known as virtual wall or virtual fence, has been significantly intensified in the post-9/11 era. It is now a component of policy preferred by some countries in Europe and North America in response to trans-national security threats. Josiah Heyman distinguishes between two meanings of this virtual system — one narrower and one broader. The narrower meaning of the virtual wall refers to the use of advanced surveillance and computer technologies in border law enforcement by utilizing, for example, ground-level radar to detect the movement of persons and to define their orientation in the vicinity of the border. More broadly, the virtual fence, according to Heyman, points to the amassing of police forces, including military and intelligence agencies, in the border region.[24] Virtual fences in the narrow sense is a first-generation application of military technology in the border-control system which has been shown to be ineffective against smugglers' and irregular immigrants' intelligent use of developed technology and different styles of camouflage. The broader meaning refers to the total virtual militarization of the border to detect with high accuracy all kind of cross-border infiltrations around the clock and regardless of weather conditions.

The search for technological solutions to border control has been present in the debate over new immigration laws adopted by the U.S. in recent years. The Border Protection, Antiterrorism, and Illegal Immigration Control Act of 2005 (H.R.4437), passed by the House in December 2005, and the Comprehensive Immigration Reform Act of 2006 (S. 2611), passed by the Senate in May 2006, both have provisions requiring implementation of new technologies to support border-control efforts at and between ports of entry, particularly along the U.S.-Mexican border.[25]

The U.S. virtual border fence is largely linked to the "Secure Border Initiative" (SBI) launched by the Department of Homeland Security in November 2005. Through the SBI, the DHS intended to enhance surveillance technologies, increase staffing levels, enforce immigration

---

24 Josiah McC. Heyman, "Constructing a Virtual Wall: Race and Citizenship in U.S.-Mexico Border Policing", *Journal of the Southwest*, Vol. 50, No. 3 (2008), p. 305.

25 Rey Koslowski, "Immigration Reforms and Border Security Technologies", *Border Battles: The U.S. Immigration Debates*. New York: Social Science Research Council (2006), http://borderbattles.ssrc.org/Koslowski

laws and improve the physical infrastructure along the U.S. borders with Mexico and Canada[26] in order to prevent trans-national security threats and reduce irregular immigration. A part of SBI, the Secure Border Initiative Network (SBInet), is a multibillion dollar program initiated in 2006 that involves the acquisition, development, integration, deployment, operation and maintenance of surveillance technologies to create a virtual fence along the border, as well as command, control, communications and intelligence (C3I) technologies to create a picture of the border in command centers and vehicles.[27] The primary goal of SBInet is to strengthen DHS's ability to control thousands of miles of American international frontier.

The U.S. virtual border fence was very costly financially. According to the U.S. Government Accountability Office, for fiscal years 2006 through 2009, the SBI program received about USD 3.6 billion in appropriated funds. Of this amount, about USD 2.4 billion has been allocated to complete approximately 670 miles of vehicle and pedestrian fencing along the roughly 2,000 miles of border between the United States and Mexico.[28] Adam Comis, the Press Secretary for the House Homeland Security Committee, stated that the cost of the entire south-western virtual fence project (if it was not stopped) is estimated to be about USD 6.7 billion by 2014.[29]

Although the U.S. government spent much money to make a technological instead of a physical fence, the SBI did not achieve its desired results. For example, many of the sensors proved difficult to maintain in a variety of weather conditions, and they cannot differentiate animals and humans.[30] The ineffectiveness of the U.S. virtual border fence program also shows itself in other aspects. Smugglers and

26 United States Government Accountability Office, "Secure Border Initiative: DHS Needs to Strengthen Management and Oversight of Its Prime Contractor", report to Congressional Requesters (October 2010), p. 1.

27 *Ibid.*, p. 1.

28 United States Government Accountability Office, "Secure Border Initiative Fence Construction Costs" [Washington, D.C.] (29 January 2009), p. 4, http://www.gao.gov/products/GAO-09-244R

29 Arthur H. Rotstein, "Officials Ready to Build Virtual Fence Along Border", *USnews & World Report* (8 May 2009), http://www.usnews.com/science/articles/2009/05/08/officials-ready-to-build-virtual-fence-along-border

30 Rey Koslowski, "Immigration Reforms and Border Security Technologies", *Border Battles: The U.S. Immigration Debates*, http://borderbattles.ssrc.org/Koslowski

irregular immigrants developed many ways to circumvent the virtual fence along the U.S. international border, especially the one shared with Mexico. Sophisticatedly deep and long tunnels have been dug secretly under the U.S.-Mexico border and are used for smuggling drugs and immigrants. This remains one of the big challenges because if can evade control by the virtual-control system.

After the many failures of the U.S. virtual border fence, Homeland Security Secretary Janet Napolitano on 11 January 2011 cancelled the Secure Border Initiative-network (SBInet) program. Napolitano justified the decision on the basis of technical problems suffered by the program, cost overruns (USD 1 billion) and schedule delays since its inception in 2005. At the same time, Napolitano announced a "new border security technology plan" that is tailored to the technological needs of each border region, including commercially available mobile surveillance systems, unmanned aircraft systems, thermal imaging devices and tower-based remote video surveillance systems.

Trump's project, though it aims to erect a concrete wall along the entirety of the U.S.-Mexico border, will face geographical and physical challenges that will prompt the U.S. government to resort to technology as a complementary measure. It will be able to reuse the technological surveillance system that has been already been in place along the border. So, high-tech fences, at least on some parts of the border, will be among the possible options and may significantly reduce the cost of the project.

Conclusion

The U.S.-Mexico border wall marks the fault line between two different worlds. Regardless of how many billions of dollars will be spent on the further fortification and militarization of the common border, illegal cross-border activities will continue so long as there is a huge disparity in economic prosperity, political stability and social security between the two countries.

Regional integration and advanced partnerships may reduce the attractiveness of emigration, but they cannot erase the American dream from the mind of millions of Latin Americans who will continue to seek new ways to reach the America El Dorado — regularly or irregularly.

5. The Wall of Western Sahara[1]

All military walls in history were originally built with a protective function to keep out invaders. China's Great Wall, the most famous and the longest manmade structure in the world, was built for defensive and protective purposes, to safeguard and unify the Chinese territory and empire. Also, in ancient civilizations, the high walls surrounding old cities were constructed as fortifications to defend the people from potential aggressors. However, modern international walls and fences are differentiated from each other according to their specific contexts and purposes. Some border walls are strictly defensive and military fortifications; others are considered to demarcate borders between two or more neighboring countries; others act as buffer lines between warring parties; and yet others have different roles and functions.

The Western Sahara Wall (also known as Sand Wall, defensive wall and Berm), which was built by Morocco in the Western Sahara,[2] is one of these walls worth studying as a specific case. The Sand Wall was built in a specific international and regional context marked by a furious conflict between the two blocs during the Cold War over the control of some geo-strategic areas, including the Maghreb region.

Researchers interested in the Western Sahara issue consider the battle between Algeria and Morocco over its fate as a piece of heritage of the Cold War, which had intensified the struggle for regional hegemony.

---

1   This chapter is drawn, with permission from the publisher, from: "The Sahara Wall: Status and Prospects", *Journal of Borderlands Studies*, Vol. 27, No. 2 (2012), pp. 199–212.

2   I use in this chapter the terms "Sahara" and "Western Sahara" interchangeably.

   https://doi.org/10.11647/OBP.0121.06

As noted by William Zartman, "by the end of 1984, the Western Saharan conflict had lost its specific focus on a piece of land and had become a clash of alliance in the Maghreb".[3] In this context, characterized by the unconditional support provided by some socialist bloc countries (mainly Algeria, Libya and Cuba) to POLISARIO,[4] Morocco had no choice but to build a defensive wall in order to impose its conditions on the battlefield.

The Advisory Opinion rendered on 6 October 1975 by the International Court of Justice remains one of the key international legal bases to which Morocco refers in its policy towards the Western Sahara. This Advisory Opinion acknowledged that there were legal ties of allegiance between the Western Sahara territory and the Kingdom of Morocco at the time of colonization by Spain. The attachment of the population to the central power (Sultans, Princes, Kalifas) during Islamic history was based especially on religious and temporal ties of the allegiance (*beyâa*), which was considered as a contract between the population and the governor.

It is noteworthy that the notion of sovereignty that had been practiced in the Arab and Muslim World differed from "Westphalian sovereignty" that emerged in Europe following the end of the Thirty Years' War in 1648. Even if the system of Westphalian sovereignty — based on territoriality — has dominated international relations from that time forward, it could not be applied retrospectively to earlier nations that had known a specific government and administration adapted to their cultural, political and social environment.

Arguably, the construction of the Western Sahara Wall is absolutely the most important military decision made by Morocco throughout the history of this issue because of its significant subsequent results not only at a military level but also because it has many considerable political and diplomatic consequences.

Moroccan Armed Forces began the construction of the Berm in 1981 through a series of steps. The project ended in April 1987 after more

---

3   William Zartman, *Ripe for Resolution: Conflict and Intervention in Africa*. New York: Oxford University Press, 1989, pp. 70–71.

4   POLISARIO is an acronym for the Popular Front for the Liberation of Saguia el Hamra and Rio de Oro, founded in Zouerate (Mauritania) on 29 April 1973 with the purpose of obtaining independence for Western Sahara.

than 2,200 kilometers had been built. The berm is made up of six walls which were successively built as following periods:

- 1st wall (Aug 1980–Jun 1982): 500 kilometers
- 2nd wall (Dec 1983–Jan 1984): 300 kilometers
- 3rd wall (Apr 1984–May 1984): 320 kilometers
- 4th wall (Dec 1984–Jan 1985): 380 kilometers
- 5th wall (May–Sep 1985): 670 kilometers
- 6th wall (Feb–Apr 1987): 550 kilometers

The berm is supported at regular intervals by observation points, support points, artillery support, underground shelters of soldiers and radar and electronic sensors systems to detect adversary vehicles. Reserve forces have been positioned behind the wall, ready to retaliate if attacked.[5] By the time the wall was completely erected, the battle in the Western Sahara had completely changed in favor of Moroccan military strategy.

Since the present and future of the Sahara Wall is tied closely to those of Western Sahara itself, before approaching the status and prospects of the Sahara Berm it is important to understand its historical origins.

A Glance at the Western Sahara Issue

This section aims to highlight both the historical ties between Morocco and the Western Sahara region and the progress of this issue in the framework of the United Nations.

The Western Sahara Region's Historical Ties to Morocco

Throughout history, the Sahara has been the strategic depth of the Moroccan State. The rootedness of the Western Sahara in Morocco results from uninterrupted continuity of a ruling dynasty, many of whom originated from the Sahara. History books overflow with indications of the ties between the Sahrawi tribes and the Moroccan state. These

---

5   Khadija Mohsen-Finan, "Murs de défense au Sahara occidental", *Études*, Vol. 400, No. 2004 (January 2004), p. 94.

ties reflected the concept of sovereignty as it was practiced during the era of Islamic rule and are consistent with the pattern of nomadic life in the Sahara, which is characterized by permanent mobility and travel, not conducive to the establishment of a fixed administration. Thus, one could not adopt the concept of territorial sovereignty — as developed in Europe after the Treaty of Westphalia in 1648 — as a standard by which to prove or deny legal ties between Western Sahara and Morocco, since these had been developed in a different political, economic and social context.

The history of the Sahara confirms that Moroccan sultans and kings have exercised various forms of authority associated with internal and external sovereignty over this region. With regard to internal sovereignty, many historical documents show that the sultan has always practiced functions related to legislative, executive and spiritual authorities.

Legislative activities, exercised by the sultan, were not limited only to sultani *dahirs* (decrees), but extended to economic activity through the control of trade and production, in particular with regard to fishing — the monopoly of which was generally reserved for the sultan's subjects, except in the case of special concessions for foreigners. They also extended administration of the ports in order to open and close them to foreign trade according to requirements of national policy. The sultan's legislative authority also related to raw materials and fiscal matters through the assessment, imposition and collection of taxes and duties.[6]

Moroccan sultans practiced executive authority in the Western Sahara region through *dahirs*, as they did in the legislative field. That was the means by which they appointed and dismissed the *caids* to whom they entrusted responsibility for the government of a region, on a coast or across a group of tribes. The *caids* are, according to the etymological meaning of the term, military commanders who also have administrative functions. The title of *caid* did not tend to be strictly an honorary one, as has been alleged.[7] It is a practice in a number of countries, in the absence of a centralized authority, to choose persons

---

6   ICJ Advisory Opinion of October 16th, 1975, on the Western Sahara, Individual Opinion of Fouad Ammoun (Vice-President), p. 84/93, http://www.icj-cij.org/files/case-related/61/061-19751016-ADV-01-04-EN.pdf

7   *Ibid.*, p. 85/93.

to govern who have the qualifications which enable them to make their authority felt and to carry out necessary tasks.[8] Morocco submitted five of those *dahirs* that showed the administrative and political linkage of the regions of Western Sahara to Morocco to the ICJ in 1975. It is the *dahirs* in documents 4, 5 and 8 which appoint *caids* over the Sahara tribes of the Tidrareen and Oulad Tidrareen, whose nomadic migration routes extend over the whole of Western Sahara, according to Mauritania's maps numbers 2 and 3 and go beyond Cabo Bojador; the dahir in document 4 also appoints the *caid* with authority over the Saharan Tekna, whose nomadic migration route extends to the northern part of the Sahara, or the Sakiet El Hamra, according to map number 3.[9]

Many European historians have agreed on the continuous and persistent link between the Western Sahara region and Morocco. Fouad Ammoun referred to five of those historians — a Frenchman, Vernet; and four Spaniards, Domenech Lafuente, Seco de Lucena, Huici and Romeu — who inspired great confidence with regard to the facts supporting the Moroccan case.[10]

The documents relied upon by Morocco show international recognition of Moroccan territorial sovereignty over the Western Sahara region. Those documents concern bilateral conventions and treaties which Morocco held with some states, notably the treaty with Spain of 1767, and treaties of 1836, 1856 and 1861 with the United States, Great Britain and Spain, respectively. Provisions of these deal with the rescue and safety of mariners shipwrecked on the Coast of Wad Noun or in its vicinity.[11] One of these significant international accords is the Franco-German exchange of letters of 1911 — appended to the Agreement between France and Germany of 4 November 1911 — which expressed the understanding of the parties that "Morocco comprises all that part of northern Africa which is situated between Algeria, French West Africa, and the Spanish colony of Rio de Oro".[12] Morocco has presented this document as clear recognition by those powers of Moroccan sovereignty over the Sakiet El Hamra as an integral part of its territory.

---

8   *ibid.*

9   *Ibid.*, p. 83/93

10   *Ibid.*, pp. 86/78–94/86.

11   For further details about these conventions see the ICJ Advisory Opinion of 16 October 1975 on the Western Sahara, p. 51.

12   *Ibid.*, p. 124, p. 41.

Although sovereignty in Islamic history had taken different dimensions, it can be generally summarized as "spiritual and temporal authority". Spiritual and religious ties had been its most important aspects. Allegiance (*beyâa*) based on religious elements was expressed by tribes and inhabitants of the Sahara region to the Moroccan central authority. Religious and spiritual dimensions gave legal force to the allegiance, and the population's belief in its obligation guaranteed the people's respect of its requirements even if the state could not extend its material authority to them. This fact explains why an important number of provinces remained subordinate to the central Islamic state for a long time despite the absence of any tangible administrative or military aspect of sovereignty that subjugated them.

Since independence in 1956, Morocco, based on the continued subordination of the Western Sahara region to its territory, has spared no effort in completing its territorial integrity, which was torn apart by progressive multinational colonization from 1884 when Spanish colonization began. Before 1956, the Moroccan people used various means, including armed struggle, for liberation from colonialism. However, the formal declaration of independence in that year made Morocco fall back slowly to rely on diplomatic and political means, such as direct negotiations and UN instruments, to complete its territorial integrity. Due to its exposure to multinational colonization and the competing interests of colonial powers, Morocco was unable to recover all of its territory at once in 1956. This did not prevent the country from declaring independence and gaining international recognition as provided in international law.

The 1960 Declaration on the Granting of Independence to Colonial Countries and Peoples stipulated in paragraph 3 that "inadequacy of political, economic, social or educational preparedness should never serve as a pretext for delaying independence".[13] Nevertheless, this did not mean that Morocco had given up the territories that remained under occupation in the north and south. In fact, the declaration of Morocco's independence in 1956 did not constitute a break with the colonial past because of the continued presence of Spanish colonies in important parts of Moroccan territory.

---

13   The Declaration on the Granting of Independence to Colonial Countries and
     Peoples, U.N. General Assembly Resolution 1514 (XV) of 14 December 1960.

Even though Morocco was able to retrieve some parts of its national territory — such as Tarfaya and the Sidi Ifni regions, which it regained respectively in 1958 and 1969 by a bilateral agreement with Spain — the Sakia El Hamra and Río de Oro regions, or what is known internationally as the "Western Sahara", have been long considered as a major obstacle to the normalization of Moroccan-Spanish relations. The Spanish government insists on individual initiatives to settle the fate of the province and to withdraw from it. This has become the main obstacle to achieving the Maghreb integration.

In addition to Spain, Algeria tried with all its strength, during this period, to prevent Morocco from achieving complete independence and reintegrating the Western Sahara region into Moroccan territory. Algeria based its position on the principle of *uti possidetis* (i.e. the principle of inviolability of borders inherited from colonization), ignoring the fact that the Western Sahara has never been separated from Moroccan territory in the past. The principle of *uti possidetis* dates back to Roman times and takes its name from the Latin phrase *"uti possidetis, ita possideatis"*, which means "as you possess, so may you possess". The modern application of the *uti possidetis* doctrine emerged after the decolonization of Latin America in the early nineteenth century. This doctrine was summarized in the 1922 arbitral award by the Swiss Federal Council that settled the territorial claim between Colombia and Venezuela. It described *uti possidetis* as "the basis of South American public law:

> [...] The principle laid down the rule that the boundaries of the newly established republics would be the frontiers of the Spanish provinces which they were succeeding. This general principle offered the advantage of establishing the general rule that in law no territory of Old Spanish America was without an owner [...]. The principle also had the advantage [...] of doing away with boundary disputes between the new states.[14]

---

14   James Brown Scott, "The Swiss Decision in the Boundary Dispute between Colombia and Venezuela", *American Journal of International Law*, Vol. 16, No. 3 (1922), pp. 428–29, cited in Paul R. Hensel, Michael E. Allison and Ahmed Khanani, "Territorial Integrity Treaties, *Uti Possidetis*, and Armed Conflict over Territory", paper presented at the 2006 Shambaugh Conference on "Building Synergies: Institutions and Cooperation in World Politics" [University of Iowa] (October 13, 2006).

In summary, the *uti possidetis* principle is a legal principle that provides that successor states accept international boundaries set by predecessor regimes.

At the beginning of twentieth century, Latin America abandoned the *uti possidetis* principle because "it was found to be too restrictive on States there in rectifying obvious errors and injustices" and "there was often confusion over the location of provinces and other subdivisions of colonial control and thus over which successor State had the right to the territories in question". Furthermore, "the principle could not be applied to adjacent territories which had been governed under different colonial regimes".[15] This has always been the attitude of the Moroccan government — amongst others — towards the principle, particularly if it involved the creation of states that, before colonization, had no status in international law.[16]

In the African context, the principle of *uti possidetis* has been adopted implicitly. For example, the resolution adopted by the Summit of the Organization of African Unity (OAU) in July 1964 in Cairo stipulated that all member states "pledge themselves to respect the borders existing on their achievement of national independence". This statement does not mean in any way that the principle of *uti possidetis* can be applied in all cases since it refers only to "national independence" excluding the independence of a part of national territory. Algeria is one of the African countries that has hugely benefited from the implementation of this principle and it has strongly defended it because "it is extremely difficult to define a pre-colonial Algerian State with the same territorial extent as is the case with modern Algeria".[17] It was very difficult in the 1960s to settle Morocco-Algerian disputes over some contiguous regions without resorting to the principle of *uti possidetis*. Although the application of this principle was not equitable for Morocco, it had demonstrated a great will to make significant territorial concessions in order to create a stable Maghreb. In the case of the Western Sahara issue, although Algeria was anxious to apply the principle in defining

---

15   George Joffe, "The International Court of Justice and the Western Sahara Dispute",
      in *War and Refugees: The Western Sahara Conflict*, Richard Lawless and Laila Monahan
      (Eds.). London and New York: Pinter Publishers, 1987, p. 17.
16   *Ibid.*
17   *Ibid.*

an entity different from Morocco in the region, Morocco had been most unwilling to do so again, if for no other reason than the simple fact that the colonial regimes involved were very different and reflected different colonial approaches rather than any inherent differences in the nature of the contiguous territories involved.[18]

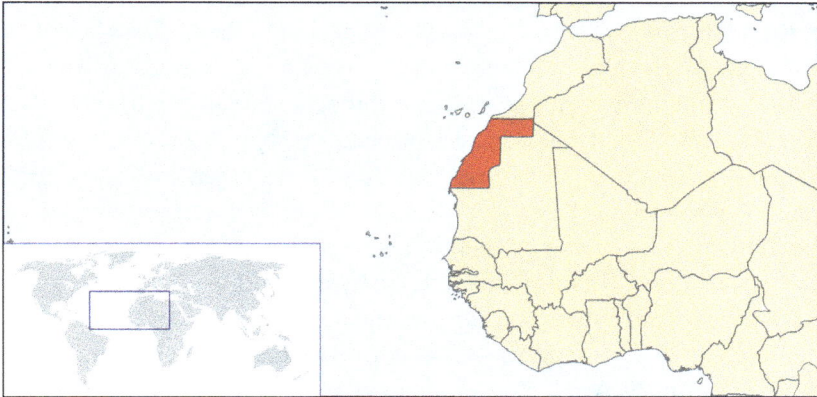

Fig. 5.1 Location of the Western Sahara. Map by Rei-artur, CC BY-SA 3.0.[19]

The UN and the Western Sahara Issue

Before Spanish withdrawal from the Western Sahara region in 1975, the UN had adopted some resolutions concerning the region. Resolution 2072 (XX), adopted by the General Assembly on 16 December 1965, called upon Spain to end its colonization of Sidi Ifni and the Sahara; and Resolution 2229 (XXI), adopted by the General Assembly on 20 December 1966, recommended negotiations for the recovery of Sidi Ifni and called upon Spain to hold a referendum on the issue of the Western Sahara.

The Advisory Opinion given by the International Court of Justice on 16 October 1975 was a turning point in the modern history of the Western Sahara region. The ICJ concluded that Western Sahara (Rio de Oro and Sakiet El Hamra) at the time of colonization by Spain was not a territory belonging to no one (*terra nullius*) and that legal ties

---

18   *Ibid.*, p. 18.
19   Source: https://commons.wikimedia.org/wiki/File%3ALocationWesternSahara.svg

existed between this territory and both the Kingdom of Morocco and the Mauritanian entity. Despite disagreement about the interpretation of the ICJ Advisory Opinion, it constituted the international legal framework for all Moroccan initiatives that seek to find a solution to the Western Sahara issue because it confirmed the existence of the political, legal and spiritual attachment of the inhabitants of the Western Sahara, on the basis of the ties of allegiance (*beyâa*) shown throughout history.

Although, the United Nations had played a very modest role in the question of the Western Sahara during the Cold War era, immediately after the end of that period the UN began to play a more active role. This was reflected in some important decisions taken by the Security Council concerning Western Sahara and other international issues. This new interaction can be seen in the action of the UN to give special importance to the Western Sahara issue by presenting a set of proposals to the parties concerned, as well as by the creation of the United Nations Mission for the Referendum in Western Sahara, commonly known as MINURSO on 29 April 1991. This new role for the UN was further reinforced by the direct sponsorship of negotiations between Morocco and the POLISARIO.[20]

Within the framework of the revival of the role of the UN in the Western Sahara issue, the Security Council unanimously adopted Resolution 690 of 29 April 1991. With this, it showed approval for the report by the Secretary-General relative to the organization of a referendum of self-determination in the Western Sahara and formally approved the creation of the MINURSO forces.[21]

The UN noticed the difficulty of putting the 1991 settlement plan into practice, and the personal envoy of the Secretary-General, James Baker, proposed another project entitled "Framework agreement on the Status of Western Sahara", known as "Baker Plan I" at the beginning of 2001. This "Framework Agreement" was characterized by its political nature, concluding that the dispute over the Western Sahara was primarily a political issue. Although it was immediately accepted by the Moroccan government as "a framework for negotiations" because it offered the population of the Western Sahara autonomy within the Moroccan state, POLISARIO rejected it on the grounds that it did not include

---

20   Said Saddiki, "The International Reference of the Moroccan Autonomy Project for the Sahara Region", *Southern Morocco News Letter* (July 2008), p. 17.

21   *Ibid.*, p. 18.

the possibility of secession of the territory; therefore, it has never been presented formally to the Security Council.

Convinced of the difficulty of applying the first plan, the former UN envoy proposed a second initiative, called "Baker Plan II", in 2003. The Security Council approved this plan in its Resolution 1495 of March 2003, which bore the title "Peace Plan for Self-Determination of the People of Western Sahara". This plan, which suffered from many practical difficulties,[22] was considered — at least by the Moroccan government — as a step backward since it once again proposed the referendum option as a solution to the Western Sahara issue. Today, the "Baker Plan II" seems largely dead; since early 2005 the UN Secretary-General has not referred to the plan in his reports concerning the situation in Western Sahara.

This is precisely why Morocco should take the initiative to present a daring project that abides by the different resolutions of the United Nations, a project called "The Moroccan Initiative for Negotiating an Autonomy Statute for the Sahara Region" (henceforth, Moroccan Autonomy Initiative).[23] The Moroccan Initiative has been welcomed unanimously by the United Nations Security Council in its Resolution 1754 of 30 April 2007. The UN expressly applauded the efforts deployed by Morocco "to move the process forward towards resolution", and describes these efforts as being "serious and credible". This praise of the Moroccan Initiative has since then been reiterated, including in subsequent Resolutions adopted by the Security Council on the situation concerning Western Sahara; namely, Resolution 1813 of 30 April 2008, Resolution 1871 of 30 April 2009, resolution 1920 of 30 April 2010, and Resolution 1979 of 27 April 2011.

Status of the Western Sahara Wall

Although the Western Sahara Wall was initially built for defensive reasons, since the beginning of the 1990s, its status has undergone an important change with the creation of the MINURSO. Military agreements signed by the two sides of the conflict have defined the status of the Berm and surrounding areas.

---

22   *Ibid.*
23   *Ibid.*

The Original Function: The Western Sahara Wall as a Defensive Military Instrument

Like other military walls in various parts of the world that were erected in times of conflict and symbolize the transition from an offensive strategy to a defensive one (by which the state or empire protects its population and sustains a *fait accompli*),[24] the Western Sahara Wall reflects a shift in the Moroccan military doctrine at the beginning of the 1980s. Morocco confirmed that the construction of the sand wall was purely for defensive purposes. Protection of civilian populations and the vital areas in Western Sahara against attacks by the POLISARIO forces was the top priority of this defensive policy.[25] Moreover, such an incremental strategy allowed Morocco to gain and secure more and more territory — a practice recommended by counter-insurgency theorists.[26]

At the time when the wall was finished, POLISARIO leaders — according to Mustapha Bouh, a former member of the POLISARIO's political bureau — had to accept that the wall imposed another kind of war on them. The Moroccans had adapted their strategy and, in turn, POLISARIO had to follow suit.27 Indeed, the construction of the Western Sahara Wall extensively affected the margin of maneuver of POLISARIO and disrupted its military capabilities, whereas it has enhanced the Moroccan military strategy on the ground and strengthened its negotiating position. This explains the significant decrease in the number of attacks carried out by POLISARIO against Moroccan forces. It was a turning point in the course of the conflict that led eventually

---

24   Alexandra Novosseloff et Frank Neisse, "La Construction des Murs, ou la Mondialisation à Rebours", *Questions internationales*, No. 33 (Septembre-Octobre 2008), p. 101.

25   Zakaria Abouddahab, "Le Mur de Défense du Sahara Occidental à L'épreuve du Droit International et de la Réalité", paper presented at the International Conference on "Fences and Walls in International Relations" organized by the Raoul-Dandurand Chair of Strategic and Diplomatic Studies in the University of Quebec, Montreal, Canada (29–30 October 2009).

26   Derek Harvey, "The Reagan Doctrine, Morocco, and the Conflict in the Western Sahara: an Appraisal of United States Policy", PhD Thesis [The University of Utah] (1988), p. 29.

27   Cited by Claude Moniquet, "The POLISARIO Front: Credible Negotiations Partner or After-Effect of the Cold War and Obstacle to a Political Solution in Western Sahara?", *European Strategic Intelligence & Security Center (ESISC)* (November 2005), p. 31.

to a cease-fire between the two sides. This situation, which disrupted the movement of POLISARIO troops, prompted POLISARIO leaders to abandon military options and enter into direct negotiations with Morocco. Arguably, the sand wall has played a double role: protection and stabilization.[28]

One of the main strategic reasons for Morocco to build a sand wall in the Western Sahara, even though it leaves an important part of the territory temporarily out of its direct control in the south and east of the Berm, is to avoid being confronted directly by the Algerian army and to avoid chasing POLISARIO guerillas into Algerian territory or violating Mauritanian sovereignty. By this military doctrine, the Moroccan army has voluntarily limited its right of pursuit in the event of POLISARIO attacks[29] and it has demarcated the battlefield. Furthermore, the wall is built in the mostly uninhabited territory in the Western Sahara. The defensive purpose of the Western Sahara Wall is clearly recognized in the Secretary-General's Report S/10/1998 of 20 October 1998 (paragraph 8 of section B, entitled "military aspects"), which stated "with its construction work for logistical and accommodation purposes nearly completed at Dakhla, the engineering support unit from Pakistan is now focusing its efforts on the establishment of the forward logistical base at Awsard and on the refurbishment of sub-sector commands east of the defensive sand wall (Berm)". Moreover, there is no report of the Secretary-General condemning the construction of the wall. In addition, no resolution of the Security Council and UN General Assembly mentions or describes the wall as "illegal".

Current Function: The Berm as a Landmark of the Cease-fire Monitoring Agreement

The current status of the Berm is defined by Military Agreement No. 1 (henceforth referred to as MA #1), which is considered as the basic legal instrument for the UN monitoring of the cease-fire in Western Sahara.

---

28   Zakaria Abouddahab, "Le Mur de Défense du Sahara Occidental à L'épreuve du Droit International et de la Réalité" (October 29–30, 2009), p. 11.

29   Claude Moniquet, "The POLISARIO Front: Credible Negotiations Partner or After-Effect of the Cold War and Obstacle to a Political Solution in Western Sahara?", p. 31.

MINURSO developed and signed MA #1[30] in December 1997 with the Royal Moroccan Army (RMA) and, in January 1998, with the Frente POLISARIO Military Forces (FPMF). One of the most important clauses of MA# 1 emphasizes that it details only activities of the military and has no provisions for civilian movements.

MA #1 divides the territory of Western Sahara into five areas. The Berm is considered to be a landmark of this demarcation. Each of the five parts has specific restrictions for the two parties' military activities.[31]

- **One 5-kilometer wide Buffer Strip to the south and east sides of the Berm:** MA #1 prohibits the entry of RMA and FPMF personnel and equipment into this area by ground or air and the firing of weapons in or over the area. It stresses that it is prohibited at all times and any infraction counts as a violation of the cease-fire.

- **Two 30-kilometer wide Restricted Areas along the Berm:** The Buffer Strip is included in the Restricted Area on the POLISARIO Front side, and the Berm is included in the Restricted Area on the RMA side. MA #1 forbids the firing of weapons and/or conducting any military training exercises, with the exception of physical training activities of unarmed personnel. Also, this agreement bans any tactical reinforcements, any redeployment or movement of troops, headquarters/units, stores, equipment, ammunition, weapons, any entry of military aircraft and any improvements of defense infrastructures. However, it notes that some exceptions apply and some activities are allowed following prior notification to or approval by MINURSO.

- **Two Areas with Limited Restrictions:** These are two remaining vast stretches of land of the Western Sahara on both sides, respectively. In these areas, all normal military activities can be carried out with the exception of the reinforcement of

---

30 See the Military Agreement No.1 on the MINURSO website as it appeared on 2 January 2010, when it was last archived using the Internet Archive Wayback Machine: http://web.archive.org/web/20090210055157/ http://www.minurso.unlb. org/monitoring.html

31 *Ibid.*

existing minefields, the laying of mines, the concentration of forces and the construction of new headquarters, barracks and ammunition storage facilities. MA #1 states also that MINURSO needs to be informed if the parties intend to conduct military exercises, including the firing of weapons of a calibre above 9 mm.

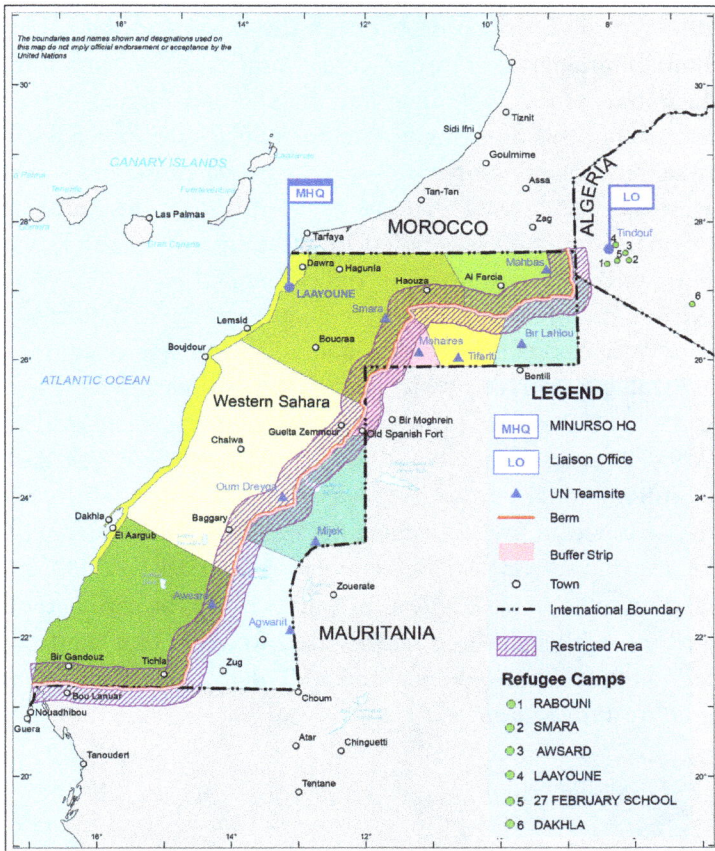

Fig. 5.2 Map made by the MINURSO based on the Military Agreement No. 1. This map drawn on 4 May 2007 shows the Operational Area of MINURSO including location of refugee camps in Tindouf.[32]

---

32 Source: the MINURSO website, as archived on the Internet Archive Wayback Machine, http://web.archive.org/web/20090210055157/http://www.minurso.unlb. org/monitoring.html

In addition to MA #1, MINURSO signed two other military agreements with the two parties separately. Military Agreement No. 2 was signed in April 1999 between the FPMF and the MINURSO with the aim of reducing the danger that represents residual mines and Unexploded ordnance (UXOs). However, the terms of this agreement do not apply to the mines and UXOs in the Buffer Strip. On the other hand, Military Agreement No. 3 was conceived within the framework of strengthening the cooperation between the RAM and the MINURSO. With humanitarian and environmental significance, it aims to reduce both the danger of residual mines and unexploded engines. It is further understood that this agreement aims to reduce the danger but not to perform a mine-cleaning operation or a large-scale research endeavor.

It is worth mentioning that the sand wall does not constitute an international border, as was noted in paragraph 56 of the Peace Plan (contained in the Report of the Secretary-General No S/2003/565 on 23 May 2003): "The Moroccan troops remaining in the Territory will [...] consist only of troops deployed in static or defensive positions along the sand wall constructed by Morocco close to the eastern and southern frontier of the Territory". Also, the report of the Secretary-General No S/1995/779 on 8 September 1995 distinguished between the Berm and the international border of Western Sahara, stating, in paragraph 25, that "as noted in my last report (S/1995/404), during consultations held by the former Special Representative in 1991, the POLISARIO Front had objected to the suggestion that its troops be confined outside the Territory, while Morocco had refused to agree that the troops be confined in the area between the sand wall (Berm) and the international border of Western Sahara".

New Functions of the Western Sahara Wall

Today, the role of the Western Sahara Wall has multiplied as a result of new phenomena in the region, especially the increase in operations made by some military groups and the growth of irregular sub-Saharan migrants crossing the Sahel and Sahara region.

Geographical features of Great Sahara, especially its immense open space and porous borders, have made the region a safe haven for some

Islamic military groups. In the last decade, they have used these to threaten countries of the region. Many attacks and kidnappings have been carried out by these groups, especially in Mauritania, South Algeria and northern areas of Niger and Mali. So, the Western Sahara Wall can be practically considered as an effectively impregnable obstacle to the movements of Islamic military groups located and acting in both the Sahara and Sahel region. This fact explains why Western Sahara remains relatively free from attacks compared with other Saharan regions.

At the same time, the Western Sahara Wall plays an important role in preventing or at least reducing the movement of irregular immigrants. This is why sub-Saharan migrants generally prefer to enter Morocco at the border east of Oujda from Algeria after they have crossed the Sahara overland, usually through Agadez in Niger and Tamanrasset in Algeria,[33] because they are aware of the difficulties of crossing into north Morocco from the south because of the Sahara Wall. This explains why cases of sub-Saharan irregular immigration mentioned periodically in reports of the UN Secretary-General on "the situation in Western Sahara" are infrequent and are limited to the south and east sides of the Berm.

The Prospects of the Western Sahara Wall

Today, the Western Sahara Wall finds itself at a crossroads because of significant developments in the Western Sahara issue, especially after the Moroccan Autonomy Initiative in 2007. This has been the subject of negotiations between the Moroccan government and POLISARIO, which started in Manhasset (U.S.) in June 2007 and have continued intermittently up to the present time. The future of the Sahara Wall depends closely on the fate of the Western Sahara issue itself. There are three potential scenarios for the future of the Western Sahara Wall, in accordance with the positions held by the conflicting parties: separation of the Western Sahara region from Morocco, success of the Moroccan Autonomy Initiative or continuation of the existing *status quo*.

---

33 For more information about the routes of irregular sub-Saharan immigration see Hein de Haas, "Irregular Migration from West Africa to the Maghreb and the European Union: An Overview of Recent Trends", *Migration Research Series*, No. 32 [Geneva: International Organization for Migration] (2008), pp. 17–49.

Separation of the Western Sahara Region: An Unrealistic Solution

The dissident thesis, adopted by Algeria and POLISARIO, focuses on the separation of the Western Sahara region and the creation of an independent state as the ultimate solution to the conflict.

The notion of "Sahrawi people" or "people of Western Sahara" has been the subject of a controversial debate which accompanied and continues to accompany the different phases of the Western Sahara issue. In fact, the populations of Western Sahara have never regarded themselves as an independent nation or people. Even if we should consider the inhabitants of the Western Sahara to constitute a people in themselves, it should be mentioned that the Sahrawi tribes are not found exclusively in the Moroccan Sahara. A great number of Sahrawis live in the entire south-west region of Algeria, from Bechar all the way to the borders between Mauritania and Mali, and in the northwest of Mauritanian territory, to the north of Mali between Timbuktu and the Algerian borders, through Taoudeni.[34]

Many international actors interested in the Western Sahara issue have been aware that the self-determination option in the Western Sahara region is unworkable without a new vision that takes into account the inadequacy of the independence option. One of the major obstacles to the referendum option is an inability to define who would be entitled to vote in such a referendum. Erik Jensen has treated this issue eloquently with the following questions: "Who is a Sahrawi, who is a western Saharan, and who should be entitled to vote in the referendum? Who should be the determining self in the fact of self-determination?"[35] The core issue, according to Jensen, has been which electorate are deemed to be qualified to vote in a referendum. For Moroccans, the right to vote must be comprehensively based on the principle of *jus sanguinis* and, thus, extended to all Saharan tribes linked to the former Spanish Sahara. For POLISARIO, the electorate should be narrowly defined in terms of *jus soli*: limited to those counted in the Spanish census of 1974.[36]

---

34 Said Saddiki, "A Reading of the Constitution 'Sahrawi Arab Democratic Republic'", *Southern Morocco Newsletter* (2008), pp. 81–82.

35 Eric Jensen, *Western Sahara: Anatomy of Stalemate*. London and Boulder, VQ: Lynne Rienner, 2005, p. 13.

36 *Ibid.*

The statement made at the Security Council on 21 April 2008 by the former Personal Envoy of the Secretary-General for Western Sahara, Peter Van Walsum, certainly reflected international awareness of the reality of the Western Sahara issue. Van Walsum considered that an independent Western Sahara is not a realistic proposition and not a reachable goal. He also urged the parties concerned to resume negotiations based on exclusion of the option of a referendum.

Furthermore, the creation of an independent state that lacks the basic conditions of viability and continuity is bound to constitute a heavy burden for the entire international community, particularly for nearby countries of the region. The risk is that such a microstate is likely to cast the entire Maghreb region into a period of trouble and uncertainty. Significantly, reservations expressed by the international community with respect to POLISARIO's separatist thesis indicate a growing awareness of the inappropriateness of creating mini-states. Such entities represent yet another heavy burden to be borne by a world that is already weighed down by political, economic and security-related problems. Today, failed states often become breeding grounds for groups involved in arms and drug trafficking, social violence and human-rights violations. To set up a failed state in the Sahara, bordering the Atlantic Ocean, would undoubtedly have a serious impact on international peace and security.

In addition, the application of such a narrow and rigid principle of self-determination, as claimed by the POLISARIO Front and its supporters, especially Algeria, implies some very dangerous political and security ramifications. Indeed, it will be at the root of some unceasing troubles in the Maghreb region, troubles which will not stop at the borders of a given country, particularly when we bear in mind the ethnic, linguistic and tribal composition of the countries of the region, mainly Algeria.[37] The diversity of the population of the Maghreb countries can be a source of strength and wealth, if properly employed. If manipulated or mismanaged, however, such population diversity could generate trouble and tension with unprecedented political and security repercussions. Such inflammation will not hold within a particular country; rather, it will consume the whole region.

---

37 Said Saddiki, "A Reading of the Constitution of the Pseudo-Sahrawi Arab Democratic Republic", p. 83.

Moroccan Autonomy Initiative: A Middle-ground Resolution

In order to break out of the impasse of the Western Sahara issue and respond to calls that have been regularly launched by the Security Council since 2004 to "the parties and States of the region to continue to cooperate fully with the United Nations to end the current impasse and to achieve progress towards a political solution", Morocco submitted a proposal for autonomy for the Sahara in 2007, within the framework of the kingdom's sovereignty and national unity. This initiative, according to the official document, is part of the endeavors made to build a modern, democratic society based on the rule of law, collective and individual freedoms and economic and social development. As such, it brings hope for a better future for the region's populations, puts an end to separation and exile and promotes reconciliation.[38]

The Moroccan Autonomy Initiative took great care to conform to the principle of self-determination, giving it a special meaning compatible with the specificity of the Western Sahara issue. The concept of autonomy is related to what is known in international law as "internal self-determination". This refers to the right to exercise political, economic and cultural autonomy within an existing state and is concretely translated into the establishment of control over the political, economic, social and cultural development of the concerned region. In Patrick Thornberry's words, "the external dimension or aspect [of self-determination] defines the status of a people in relation to another people, State or Empire, whereas the democratic or internal dimension should concern the relationship between a people and 'its own' State or government".[39] Article 5 of the Moroccan Autonomy Project falls within the latter perspective in so far as it stipulates that "the Sahara populations will themselves run their affairs democratically, through legislative, executive and judicial bodies enjoying exclusive powers. They will have the financial resources needed for the region's

---

38 Article 3 of the Moroccan Project of Autonomy.
39 Patrick Thornberry, "The Democratic or Internal Aspect of Self-determination With Some Remarks on Federalism", in *Modern Law of Self-Determination*, Christian Tomuschat (Ed.). Dordrecht: Martinus Nijhoff, 1993, p. 101.

development in all fields, and will take an active part in the nation's economic, social and cultural life".[40]

Unlike other proposed projects, including the referendum, which have encountered tremendous problems in terms of their implementation, the Moroccan Autonomy Initiative seems to be a concrete project. The Moroccan Initiative has, thanks to its realism, garnered wide international support within the Security Council and elsewhere because it is considered as a credible and realistic solution to the conflict in the Sahara.

Comparative constitutional law has been able to lift the ambiguity surrounding the definition of the notion of the autonomy statute, given that the right to self-government has resulted, in some cases, from the practical experience of autonomy statutes. At this level, three categories of autonomy statutes can be distinguished which spring from constitutional practice.[41] The first category is the one organized by the constitution of the state concerned, which gives the autonomous authority its own judiciary as well as some exclusive legislative powers. For example, this arrangement applies in the Aaland Islands of Finland, the region of Gagauzia in Moldova and other instances in Spain, Italy and Portugal. The second category is composed of the specific statutes of an official constitutional delegation and concerns the power to create laws except for its own laws. Here, working examples include Greenland and the Faeroe islands in Denmark. In contrast to the first category, the second is an example of a "fully autonomous territory", or, as Kristian Myntti described the case of Greenland, an "autonomous territory proper".[42] The third category constitutes regimes of autonomy that enjoy a specific constitutional statute whereby the attribution of ordinary administrative and judicial competence belongs to those of the central authorities concerned. The Crimea region in Ukraine falls into

---

40   Moroccan Initiative for Negotiating an Autonomy Statute for the Saharan Region, 10 April, 2007.

41   Markku Suksi, "On the Entrenchment of Autonomy", in *Autonomy: Applications and Implications*, Markku Suksi (Ed.). The Hague: Kluwer Law International, 1998, pp. 151–71.

42   Kristian Myntti, "The Beneficiaries of Autonomy Arrangements — with Special Reference to Indigenous Peoples in General and the Saami in Finland in Particular", in *ibid.*, p. 279.

this third category. According to the studies conducted by Markku Suksi (1998), only the Spanish Constitution provides for the autonomy as a claimable constitutional right (Article 2 of the Spanish Constitution),[43] whereas all other constitutions do not recognize the statute of autonomy as a constitutional right.

Hence, the Moroccan Initiative appears to be a middle-ground solution. It states in Article 29 that "the Moroccan Constitution shall be amended and the autonomy Statute incorporated into it, in order to guarantee its sustainability and reflect its special place in the country's national juridical architecture". The integration of the autonomy statute of the Western Sahara region in the constitutional text reflects, indeed, the importance given by Moroccan decision makers to this project.

As far as the competences attributed to the autonomous region are concerned, there are two cases where the exclusive competences of the central power are listed when the attributions of the autonomous region emanate from the organic or ordinary law. Otherwise, only the exclusive competences of the autonomous region are listed, which implicitly suggests that all other attributions belong to the central authority, be they exclusive to the state or in common bond with the autonomous region. In yet a third situation, one which was equally adopted by the Moroccan project, the exclusive competences of the central power and the autonomous region are laid out in a clear manner either in connection with exclusive or conjoined competence. One condition, however, is that "powers which are not specifically entrusted to a given party shall be exercised by common agreement, on the basis of the principle of subsidiarity".[44]

In addition to the above, the Moroccan project is also characterized by seeking to establish a negotiated autonomy on the basis of compromise between the parties concerned and is not imposed unilaterally by constitutional, ordinary or organic law. That is why the Moroccan government considers it as a ground for negotiations with POLISARIO, not a final version of the autonomy statute.

---

43   Article 2 of the Spanish Constitution states that "The Constitution [...] Recognizes and Guarantees the Right to Autonomy of the Nationalities and Regions which make it up and the solidarity among all of them".

44   Article 17 of the Moroccan Project of Autonomy.

Continuation of the status quo

The third possibility is that the Western Sahara Wall will perpetuate for many years, consolidating the *status quo* in the region, since there are no indications of a clear willingness from POLISARIO to compromise its position on creating an independent state in the region. This *status quo* scenario may take one of two paths:

- Continuation of the current stalemate of the Western Sahara issue that has been in place for the previous three decades.

- Implementation of an autonomy statute in the Western Sahara region unilaterally by Morocco, as a result of the failure of negotiations between the two sides that were initiated in 2007 under UN auspices.

Aware of the gravity of this scenario, some observers have warned that the collapse of negotiations between Morocco and POLISARIO will have far-reaching impacts on the future of the Western Sahara dispute and will perpetuate the *status quo*. This conclusion is associated with the rise of many voices in Morocco that call for applying the autonomy initiative unilaterally in the framework of the new Moroccan policy of advanced regionalization, which aims at improving and enhancing the competence of local authorities.

Some international and regional powers are satisfied with the maintenance of the *status quo* in the region because they benefit from the current situation. The prevailing view in the United Nations is to put an end to the problem and overcome the current stalemate. Secretary-General Ban Ki-Moon stated, in the UN report on the situation concerning Western Sahara on 14 April 2008, that the momentum developed in recent years can be maintained only by trying to find a way out of the current political impasse through realism and a spirit of compromise from both parties. He concluded that "the consolidation of the *status quo* is not an acceptable outcome of the current process of negotiations".

Conclusion

The Western Sahara issue is one of the heavy legacies of the colonization age that left Africa with arbitrary and unreasonable borders which were demarcated inequitably. Therefore, the Berm is just one aspect of a complex conflict, and it will disappear only once the original issue is brought to an ultimate and just resolution. The paradox is that the Western Sahara itself is also but one aspect of the regional system that has existed in the Maghreb region since the end of French colonialism.

Although granting an autonomy statute for the Western Sahara region is currently an equitable and realistic solution for the issue because it aims to achieve a middle-ground resolution, it cannot be separated from the nature of the current Maghreb system that is marked by competition for regional leadership. Currently, there are no indications of establishing cooperation between the two countries on border control because of three key factors: first, the continuing influence of the "deep state" and the enduring political deadlock in Algeria; second, the current structure of the Maghreb regional system and the existing balance of power in the region; and third, Algeria currently has no interest in settling the dispute. So long as the current regional system exists and the concerned international and regional powers are satisfied with the maintenance of the *status quo* in the region, there is little hope of resolving the issue.

Conclusions

The functions of international borders, as well as other components and symbols of the nation-state, have changed substantially due to the ever-changing nature of the international environment. At the inception of the nation-state, borders were viewed in military terms. Before the end of the nineteenth century, most states in Europe and North America took a more or less "hands-off" attitude towards the immigration movement. Due to the increasing number of people leaving their home countries, control over cross-border movement became a central concern of the nation-state. According to the Westphalian model of sovereignty, migration control had been the "reserved domain" of the nation-state and a quintessential act of its sovereignty. Consequently, states traditionally enjoy exclusive rights to pass immigration laws that regulate the movement of people across their borders and to decide which to admit, how many and where from.

The common denominator of new immigration policies taken by the host countries in the last two decades is the linking between immigration policy and border-control management on one hand, and between the immigration policy and security issues on the other hand. Additionally, tightening border control and enhancing judicial measures related to irregular immigration are the major means by which the immigrant-receiving countries try to assert national sovereignty. This may be seen as a response to the decline of countries' powers to control the flow of money, ideas, information and all kinds of virtual interactions in and out of their territories, which have slipped more and more outside their authority.

 https://doi.org/10.11647/OBP.0121.07

Security concerns remain a main determinant of the current border-control policies which aim at preventing infiltration of members of armed groups, irregular migration, goods smuggling, drug trafficking and other clandestine cross-border activities. In some cases, border fortification reflects the desire to impose unilaterally the *de facto* border. In addition to these declared goals, the current border fortifications, especially in the Middle East and South Asia, reflect the nature of the existing regional subsystems which are characterized by mutual suspicion and mistrust between different neighboring nations. These anarchical regional subsystems prompt governments to resort to unilateral and preventive solutions.

The nature of the existing regional subsystems — in North America, North Africa, Middle East or South Asia — is a key factor that determines the current border-control policies led especially by the receiving countries and those most threatened by transnational armed groups. Additionally, with the exception of the U.S.-Mexico border, the legacy of a colonial past and, to a lesser extent, the nation-building process have heavily influenced the border-security policies of post-colonial countries in Asia and Africa.

One of the paradoxes of "globalization" is that an increasingly interconnected and interdependent world is simultaneously marked by intensified militarization and fortification of national borders. Today, some regions — whether in North America, the Mediterranean or some Asian sub-regions — are being pulled in two different directions: one toward more complementarity and integration (e.g., NAFTA, Union for Mediterranean, ASEAN, SAARC) and another toward the erection of further tangible and intangible border barriers.

Despite relentless efforts by receiving countries to prevent unauthorized border-crossing by immigrants, drug smugglers and dissidents, these groups have not been deterred. Rather, they have adapted to the strategies designed to impede their movement, developing new ways and means to circumvent such barriers. It is argued that illegal immigration and transnational armed groups cannot be stopped solely by the erection of more walls and fences, but by comprehensive policies based especially on addressing their root causes. In some regions, unauthorized immigration has not declined as a result of tighter border control but because of the economic crisis that has hit some host countries in the last decade. Although a huge amount of money and efforts have been spent on the construction of physical barriers along various international borders or fighting lines in the post-Cold War era, the results achieved have often been less than desired.

Though military walls may reach some short-term goals by destabilizing the enemy, armed groups can adapt to the new situation by developing missiles that can exceed the height of these barriers, by digging tunnels or by penetrating the enemy lines using forged documents as has been seen in Palestine and Kashmir.

The construction of physical barriers along many borders all over the world may have revived realist conceptions of national security and sovereignty, but transitional non-state actors, as the main target of these border fortification policies, have seriously questioned whether their impact on international affairs has been neglected. Regardless of all the internal and external challenges faced by a nation-state, borders remain a meaningful symbol of national identity and continue to constitute one of the main determinants of foreign policies. Inasmuch as fortifying national borders in recent years reflects part of these challenges faced by the nation-state, it shows the capabilities of the nation-state to adapt to these new challenges.

Bibliography

Abouddahab, Zakaria. "Le Mur de Défense du Sahara Occidental à L'épreuve du Droit International et de la Réalité", paper presented at the International Conference on "Fences and Walls in International Relations", University of Quebec, Montreal, Canada (29–30 October 2009).

"Afghanistan-Pakistan: Focus on Bilateral Border Dispute", *IRIN* (30 October 2003), http://www.irinnews.org/report.aspx?reportid=20801

Akhmadov, Erkin. "Uzbekistan-Kyrgyzstan: Building a Wall", *The Central Asia-Caucasus Institute — Bi-Weekly Briefing*, Vol. 11, No. 13 (2009), pp. 16–17.

Alatout, Samer. "Walls as Technologies of Government: The Double Construction of Geographies of Peace and Conflict in Israeli Politics, 2002-Present", *Annals of the Association of American Geographers*, Vol. 99, No. 5 (2009), pp. 956–68, http://dces.wisc.edu/wp-content/uploads/sites/30/2013/08/The-Israeli-Separation-Wall-and-Technologies-of-Government-the-Double-Construction-of-Geographies-of-Peace-and-Conflict.pdf, https://doi.org/10.1080/00045600903260473

Aldrich, Robert and John Connell. *The Last Colonies*. Cambridge: Cambridge University Press, 1998, https://doi.org/10.1017/cbo9780511598920

Algazy, Joseph. "Soiled Hands, spoiled Lands", *Haaretz* (24 December 1999).

Almog, Doron. "Lessons of the Gaza Security Fence for the West Bank", *Jerusalem Issue Brief*, Jerusalem Center for Public Affairs, Vol. 4, No. 12 (2004).

Alscher, Stefan. "Knocking at the Doors of 'Fortress Europe': Immigration and Border Control in Southern Spain and Eastern Poland", working paper No. 126, Humboldt University, Berlin, Germany (November 2005).

Andreas, Peter. *Border Games: Policing the US-Mexico Divide*. Ithaca, NY and London: Cornell University Press, 2000.

Andreas, Peter. "Redrawing the Line: Borders and Security in the Twenty-first Century", *International Security*, Vol. 28, No. 2 (2003), pp. 78–111, https://doi.org/10.1162/016228803322761973

"Annual Report 2007–2008 of the Union Ministry of Home Affairs". New Delhi: Government of India, 2008, http://mha.nic.in/sites/upload_files/mha/files/pdf/ar0708-Eng.pdf

Ashkar, Riad. "The Syrian and Egyptian Campaigns", *Journal of Palestine Studies*, Vol. 3, No. 2 (1974), pp. 15–33, https://doi.org/10.2307/2535797

Aung, Thin Thin and Soe Myint. "India-Burma relations", *Challenges to Democratization in Burma*. Stockholm: International Institute for Democracy and Electoral Assistance, 2001, pp. 87–96.

Avnery, Uri. "First of All — the Wall Must Fall", *Gush Shalom* (30 August 2003), http://www.globalresearch.ca/articles/AVN309A.html

Babacan, Nuray. "Turkey builds 700 kilometer long wall on Syrian border", *Hurriyet Daily News* (15 June 2017), http://www.hurriyetdailynews.com/turkey-builds-700-kilometer-long-wall-on-syrian-border.aspx?PageID=238&NID=114336&NewsCatID=341

Benmelech, Efraim and Claude Berrebi. "Human Capital and the Productivity of Suicide Bombers", *Journal of Economic Perspectives*, Vol. 21, No. 3 (2007), pp. 223–38, https://doi.org/10.1257/jep.21.3.223

Bhattarai, Chandra Moni. "India-Bangladesh Border Fencing and Community Responses", conference paper, Annual International Studies Convention 2013, Delhi, India (10–12 December 2013).

Birse, Robert. "Pakistan's Afghan Border Fence Plan 'Impractical'", Reuters (27 December 2006), http://www.reuters.com/article/us-pakistan-afghan-border-idUSSP15690820061227

"Border Fencing Upsets Village Life in Moreh", *The Sangai Express* (9 May 2011), http://e-pao.net/GP.asp?src=3..100511.may11

Boswell, Christian. "The 'External Dimension' of EU Immigration and Asylum Policy", *International Affairs*, Vol. 79, No. 3 (2003), pp. 619–38, https://doi.org/10.1111/1468-2346.00326

"Burma-India Boundary", *International Boundary Study*, No. 80 (May 1968), United States State Department, Bureau of Intelligence and Research, http://fall.fsulawrc.com/collection/LimitsinSeas/IBS080.pdf

Calavita, Kitty. "Immigration, Law, and Marginalization in a Global Economy: Notes from Spain", *Law & Society Review*, Vol. 32, No. 3 (1998), pp. 529–66, https://doi.org/10.2307/827756

Calavita, Kitty. *Immigration at the Margins: Law, Race and Exclusion in Southern Europe*. New York: Cambridge University Press, 2005, https://doi.org/10.1017/cbo9780511493942

Carling, Jørgen. "Migration Control and Migrant Fatalities at the Spanish-African Borders", *International Migration Review*, Vol. 41, No. 2 (2007), pp. 316–43, https://doi.org/10.1111/j.1747-7379.2007.00070.x

Carol, Steven. *Middle East Rules of Thumb*: *Understanding the Complexities of the Middle East*. New York: iUniverse, 2008.

"Census Data 2011", Office of the Registrar General & Census Commissioner, Ministry of Home Affairs, Government of India, http://www.censusindia.gov.in/2011-Common/CensusData2011.html

Ceriani, Pablo, Fernández Bessa Cristina, Manavella Alejandra, Picco Valeria and Rodeiro Luis. "Report on the Situation on the Euro-Mediterranean Borders", Work package 9, University of Barcelona (27 April 2009), https://chabaka2000.files.wordpress.com/2014/03/2009-report-on-the-situation-on-the-euro-mediterranean-borders.pdf

Chandran, D. Suba and P. G. Rajamohan. "Soft, Porous or Rigid? Towards Stable Borders in South Asia", South Asian Survey, Vol. 14, No. 1 (2007), pp. 117–28, https://doi.org/10.1177/097152310701400109

"China Boosts North Korea Border Fence", *The China Post* (31 March 2011), http://www.chinapost.com.tw/china/national-news/2011/03/31/296806/China-boosts.htm

"China Erects Massive Fence on N. Korean Border After Test", *The World Tribune* (25 October 2006), http://www.worldtribune.com/worldtribune/06/front2454034.086111111.html

Coleman, Mathew. "Immigration Geopolitics beyond the Mexico-US Border", *Antipode*, Vol. 39, No. 1 (2007), pp. 54–76, https://doi.org/10.1111/j.1467-8330.2007.00506.x

Convergence and Employment: *The Spanish National Reform Program*, Spanish Government, Office of the Presidency of the Spanish Government. Madrid: Ministerio de la Presidencia, 2005.

Daly, Matthew and Alicia A. Caldwell, "Zinke: Border Wall 'Complex', Faces Geographic Challenges", *Washington Times* (29 March 2017), http://www.washingtontimes.com/news/2017/mar/29/zinke-border-wall-complex-faces-geographic-challen/

Das, Pushpita. "The India-Bangladesh Border: A Problem Area for Tomorrow", working paper, Institute for Defence Studies and Analyses, New Delhi, India (8 December 2006), http://www.idsa.in/idsastrategiccomments/TheIndiaBangladeshBorder%20AProblemAreaforTomorrow_PDas_081206

Das, Pushpita. *India's Border Management*: *Select Documents*. New Delhi: Institute for Defence Studies and Analyses, 2010, http://www.idsa.in/system/files/book/book_IndiasBorderManagement.pdf

Das, Pushpita. "India-Myanmar Border Problems: Fencing Not the Only Solution". Institute for Defence Studies and Analyses, New Delhi, India (15 November 2013), http://www.idsa.in/idsacomments/IndiaMyanmarBorderProblems_pdas_151113

Datta, Sreeradha. "Security of India's Northeast: External Linkages", *Strategic Analysis*, Vol. 24, No. 8 (2000), pp. 1495–1516, https://doi.org/10.1080/09700160008455301

Davis, Mike. "The Great Wall of Capita", *Border Culture*, in Ilan Stavans (Ed.), pp. 27–29. Santa Barbara: Greenwood, 2009.

De Pinies, Jaime. *La Descolonización del Sáhara: Un Tema sin Concluir*. Madrid: Espasa crónica, 1990.

Diener, Alexander C. and Joshua Hagen. *Borderlines and Borderlands: Political Oddities at the Edge of the Nation-State*. Plymouth: Rowman & Littlefield, 2010.

Doukouré, Ounia and Helen Oger. "The EC External Migration Policy: The Case of the MENA Countries", research paper 2007/6, European University Institute, RSCAS (2007), http://cadmus.eui.eu/bitstream/handle/1814/7991/CARIM-RR_2007_06.pdf

Drago, Tito. "Spain: From the Berlin Wall to Ceuta and Melilla", *Inter Press Service* (5 October 2005), http://www.ipsnews.net/2005/10/spain-from-the-berlin-wall-to-ceuta-and-melilla/

Drew, Kate. "This is What Trump's Border Wall Could Cost", *CNBC* (26 January, 2017), http://www.cnbc.com/2015/10/09/this-is-what-trumps-border-wall-could-cost-us.html

Durrani, Mahmud Ali. "Enhancing Security through a Cooperative Border Monitoring Experiment: A Proposal for India and Pakistan", Cooperative Monitoring Center, Occasional Paper (21 July 2001).

El-Badri, Hassan, Taha El-Magdoub and Mahammed Dia El-Din Zohdy. *The Ramadan War*. Dunn Loring: T. N. Dupuy Associates, Inc., 1973.

Eshel, David. "Counter-guerrilla Warfare in South Lebanon", *Marine Corps Gazette*, No. 1 (July 1997).

Eshel, David. "The Israel-Lebanon Border Enigma", *IBRU Boundary and Security Bulletin*, Vol. 8, No. 4 (2000–2001), pp. 72–83.

Falk, Richard A. "Toward Authoritativeness: The ICJ Ruling on Israel's Security Wall", *The American Journal of International Law*, Vol. 99, No. 1 (2005), pp. 42–52, https://doi.org/10.2307/3246088

Feigenbaum, Anna. "Concrete Needs No Metaphor: Globalized Fences as Sites of Political Struggle", *Ephemera*, Vol. 10, No. 2 (2010), pp. 119–33.

Ferrer-Gallardo, Xavier. "The Spanish-Moroccan Border Complex: Processes of Geopolitical, Functional and Symbolic Rebordering", *Political Geography*, Vol. 27, No. 3 (2008), pp. 301–21, https://doi.org/10.1016/j.polgeo.2007.12.004

Freeman, Carla and Drew Thompson. "The Real Bridge to Nowhere: China's Foiled North Korea Strategy", working paper, United States Institute of Peace (22 April 2009).

Freudenstein, Roland. "Rio Odra, Rio Buh: Poland, Germany, and the Borders of Twenty-First-Century Europe", in *The Wall Around the West*: *State Borders and Immigration Controls in North America and Europe*, Peter Andreas and Timothy Snyder (Eds.). Oxford: Rowman and Littlefield, 2000.

Frisch, Felix. "Israel Plans: Tax to Be Imposed on Palestinians Who Enter Israel", *Y-net* (6 March 2003).

Furness, Shelagh. "Brave New Borderless State: Illegal Immigration and the External Borders of the EU", *IBRU Boundary and Security Bulletin* (Autumn 2000), pp. 92–103.

Ganguly, Rajat. "India, Pakistan and the Kashmir Dispute", working paper, Asian Studies Institute (1998).

Gavrilis, George. *The Dynamics of Interstate Boundaries*. New York: Cambridge University Press, 2008.

Gawrych, George W. "The 1973 Arab-Israeli War: The Albatross of Decisive", *Leavenworth Papers*, No. 21, U.S. Army Center of Military History, Washington (1996).

Ghasmilee, Sara. "Iran Builds Security Fence Along Pakistan Border", *Alarabia News* (16 April 2011), http://english.alarabiya.net/articles/2011/04/16/145643.html

Gold, Peter. *A Stone in Spain's Shoe*: *The Search for the Solution for the Problem of Gibraltar*. Liverpool: Liverpool University Press, 1994, https://doi.org/10.5949/upo9781846317262

Gold, Peter. *Europe or Africa?*: *A Contemporary Study of the Spanish North African Enclaves of Ceuta and Melilla*. Liverpool: Liverpool University Press, 2000, https://doi.org/10.5949/upo9781846313066

Gonzalez, Lydia E. and Richard M. Bride. "Fortress Europe: Fear of Immigration? Present and Future of Immigration Law and Policy in Spain", *UC Davis Journal of International Law and Policy*, Vol. 6, No. 2 (2000), pp. 153–91.

Greenberg, Hanan. "Army Building New Gaza Barrier", *Y-net* (4 April 2005), http://www.ynetnews.com/articles/0,7340,L-3072620,00.html

Haas, Hein de. "Irregular Migration from West Africa to the Maghreb and the European Union: An Overview of Recent Trends", *Migration Research Series*, No. 32, Geneva: International Organization for Migration (2008).

Haddal, Chad C., Yule Kim, and Michael John Garcia. *Border Security*: *Barriers along the U.S. International Border*, RL33659. Washington, D.C.: Congressional Research Service (16 March 2009).

Harel, Amos. "Cost of Fence Could Rise to NIS 15 Million per Kilometre", *Haaretz* (8 April 2004).

Hartman, Ben. "First Permanent Section of Sinai Border Fence Completed", *The Jerusalem Post* (2 June 2011), http://www.jpost.com/Defense/First-permanent-section-of-Sinai-border-fence-completed

Harvey, Derek. "The Reagan Doctrine, Morocco, and the Conflict in the Western Sahara: An Appraisal of United States Policy", PhD Thesis, The University of Utah (1988).

Hassner, Ron and Jason Wittenberg. "Barriers to Entry: Who Builds Fortified Boundaries and Are They Likely to Work?" paper presented at the annual meeting of the American Political Science Association, Toronto, Canada (3–6 September 2009).

Hazarika, Sanjoy. *Rites of Passage: Border Crossings, Imagined Homelands, India's East and Bangladesh*. New Delhi: Penguin Books, 2000.

Helfont, Tally. "Egypt's Wall with Gaza and the Emergence of a New Middle East Alignment", *ORBIS*, Vol. 54, No. 3 (2010), pp. 426–40, https://doi.org/10.1016/j.orbis.2010.04.008

Herzl, Theodore. *The Jewish State: An Attempt at a Modern Solution of the Jewish Question*, 6th ed. (New York: Maccabean Publishing Co., 1904).

Herzl, Theodore. *Der Judenstaat* (Leipzig and Vienna: M. Breitenstein's Verlags-Buchhandlung, 1896).

Heyman, Josiah McC. "Constructing a Virtual Wall: Race and Citizenship in U.S.-Mexico Border Policing", *Journal of the Southwest*, Vol. 50, No. 3 (2008), pp. 305–34, https://doi.org/10.1353/jsw.2008.0010

Hoefer, Michael, Rytina, Nancy and Bryan C. Baker, "Estimates of the Unauthorized Immigrant Population Residing in the United States: January 2009", U.S. Department of Homeland Security, Office of Immigration Statistics (January 2010), http://www.dhs.gov/xlibrary/assets/statistics/publications/ois_ill_pe_2009.pdf

"Humanitarian Impact of the West Bank Barrier", a report to the Humanitarian Emergency Policy Group (HEPG), compiled by the United Nations Office for Coordination of Humanitarian Affairs (OCHA) and the United Nations Relief and Works Agency for Palestine Refugees (UNRWA) in the occupied Palestinian territory, No. 6 (January 2006), https://unispal.un.org/DPA/DPR/unispal.nsf/0/1FE4606B31BC49748525713900575924

"Humanitarian Impact of the West Bank Barrier on Palestinian Communities", Office for the Coordination of Humanitarian Affairs (OCHA) United Nations Relief and Works Agency for Palestine Refugees in the Near East (UNRWA), Report No. 7 (June 2007), https://unispal.un.org/DPA/DPR/unispal.nsf/0/1FE4606B31BC49748525713900575924

Huntington, Samuel. "The Clash of Civilizations", *Foreign Affairs*, Vol. 72, No. 3 (1993), pp. 22–49, https://doi.org/10.2307/20045621

"IBMS Installed at Pak-Afghan Border", *Dawn News* (28 August 2012), http://dawn.com/2012/08/28/ibms-installed-at-pak-afghan-border

"ICJ Advisory Opinion of 16 October 1975, on the Western Sahara", Individual Opinion of Fouad Ammoun (Vice-President), International Court of Justice, pp. 84/93, http://www.icj-cij.org/files/case-related/61/6197.pdf

"India, Burma to Fence the Border", *Mizzima News* (17 May 2003), http://www.burmalibrary.org/TinKyi/archives/2003-05/msg00018.html

"Integrated Border Control in the Islamic Republic of Iran (IRNI50)", United States Office on Drugs and Crime project document.

International Migration Outlook 2010. Paris: SOPEMI, OECD, 2010, http://www.oecd.org/els/mig/internationalmigrationoutlook2010.htm

International Migration Report 2015: *Highlights*. New York: United Nations Department of Economic and Social Affair, 2016, http://www.un.org/en/development/desa/population/migration/publications/migrationreport/docs/MigrationReport2015_Highlights.pdf

"Iran Building 'Anti-terror' Fence on Pakistan Border" (15 April 2011), http://www.defence.pk/forums/world-affairs/103682-iran-building-anti-terror-fence-pakistan-border.html

"Iran's Eastern Borders to be Sealed off by 2015 to Prevent Smuggling, Infiltration", *Al-Arabiya News* (2 July 2012), http://www.alarabiya.net/articles/2011/07/02/155830.html

"Israel and the Occupied Territories: The issue of Settlements Must be Addressed According to International Law", Amnesty International (8 September 2003).

"Israel and the Occupied Territories: The Place of the Fence/Wall in International Law", Amnesty International (19 February 2004), https://www.amnesty.org/en/documents/MDE15/016/2004/en/

Jamwal, N. S. "Border Management: Dilemma of Guarding the India-Bangladesh Border", *Strategic Analysis*, Vol. 28, No. 1 (2004), pp. 5–36, https://doi.org/10.1080/09700160408450116

Jaspal, Zafar Nawaz. "Threat of Extremism & Terrorist Syndicate beyond FATA", *Journal of Political Studies*, Vol. 1, No. 2 (2010), pp. 19–49.

Jensen, Eric. *Western Sahara*: *Anatomy of Stalemate*. London: Lynne Rienner, 2005.

Joffe, George. "The International Court of Justice and the Western Sahara Dispute", in *War and Refugees*: *The Western Sahara Conflict*, Richard Lawless and Laila Monahan (Ed.). London: Pinter, 1987, pp. 16–30.

Johnson, Thomas H. and M. Chris Mason. "No Sign until the Burst of Fire: Understanding the Pakistan-Afghanistan Frontier", *International Security*, Vol. 32, No. 4 (2008), pp. 41–77, https://doi.org/10.1162/isec.2008.32.4.41

Joseph, Jolin and Vishnu Narendran. "Neither Here nor There: An Overview of South-South Migration from both ends of the Bangladesh-India Migration Corridor", working paper No. 569, *Migration Literature Review*, No. 1 (October 2013).

Joshi, Binoo. "India-Pakistan Border Fence Affecting Wildlife", *Indo-Asian News Service* (6 February 2008), http://twocircles.net/node/78400

Kanchan, L. "Negotiating Insurgencies", *Faultlines* (11 April 2002), http://www.satp.org/satporgtp/publication/faultlines/volume11/Article7.htm

Kansakar, Vidya Bir Singh. "Nepal-India Open Border: Prospects, Problems and Challenges", *Institute of Foreign Affairs*, Kathmandu, Nepal (2001), http://www.fes.de/aktuell/focus_interkulturelles/focus_1/documents/19.pdf

Karlekar, Hiranmay. *Bangladesh: The Next Afghanistan?* New Delhi: Sage Publication, 2005.

Keinon, Herb".P.M. Sets Summer as Completion Date for Egypt Fence", *Jerusalem Post* (15 March 2011), http://www.jpost.com/Defense/PM-sets-summer-2012-as-completion-date-for-Egypt-fence

Khan, Zahid Ali. "Balochistan Factor in Pak-Iran Relations: Opportunities and Constraints", *South Asian Studies*, Vol. 27, No. 1 (2012), pp. 121–40.

Knickmeyer, Ellen. "Egypt to Bolster Gaza Border" *Washington Post* (7 January 2008), http://www.washingtonpost.com/wp-dyn/content/article/2008/01/06/AR2008010602055.html

Koslowski, Rey. "Immigration Reforms and Border Security Technologies", *Border Battles: The U.S. Immigration Debates*. New York: Social Science Research Council, 2006, http://borderbattles.ssrc.org/Koslowski

Kuppuswamy, C. S. "Indo-Myanmar Relations — A Review", working paper No. 2043, South Asia Analysis Group (November 2006).

Lagerquist, Peter. "Fencing the Last Sky: Excavating Palestine after Israel's 'Separation Wall'", *Journal of Palestine Studies*, Vol. 33, No. 2 (2004), pp. 5–35, https://doi.org/10.1525/jps.2004.33.2.5

Laithangbam, Iboyaima. "Fencing along Manipur-Myanmar Border Progressing", *The Hindu* (8 September 2010), http://www.thehindu.com/news/national/article619798.ece

Lakshmi, Rama. "India's Border Fence Extended to Kashmir Country Aims to Stop Pakistani Infiltration", *The Washington Post* (30 July 2003), http://antigenocide.org/images/India-30-Jul-03-India_s_Border_Fence_Extended_to_Kashmir.pdf

Lein, Yehezkel. "Behind the Barrier: Human Rights Violations As a Result of Israel's Separation Barrier", position paper, Trans. Zvi Shulman, *B'Tselem* (March 2003), https://www.btselem.org/download/200304_behind_the_barrier_eng.pdf

Lewis, Martin W. "The Iran-Pakistan Border Barrier", *GeoCurrents* (13 May 2011), http://geocurrents.info/geopolitics/the-iran-pakistan-border-barrier

Lindsey, Ursula. "Egypt's Wall", *Middle East Research and Information Project* (1 February 2010), http://www.merip.org/mero/mero020110

Lintner, Bertil. *Burma in Revolt: Opium and Insurgency Since 1948*. Boulder: Westview Press, 1994.

MacFarlane, Neil Stina Torjesen, and Christina Wille. "An Anomaly in Central Asia? Small Arms in Kyrgyzstan", in *Small Arms Survey 2004: Right at Risk*, UNLIREC (Ed.). Oxford: Oxford University Press, 2004, pp. 309–27, http://www.smallarmssurvey.org/fileadmin/docs/A-Yearbook/2004/en/Small-Arms-Survey-2004-Chapter-10-EN.pdf

Makovsky, David. "How to Build a Fence", *Foreign Affairs*, Vol. 83, No. 2 (2004), pp. 50–64, https://doi.org/10.2307/20033902

Mara'i, Tayseer and Usama R. Halabi. "Life under Occupation in the Golan Heights", *Journal of Palestine Studies*, Vol. 22, No. 1 (1992), pp. 78–93, https://doi.org/10.1525/jps.1992.22.1.00p0166n

Mark, Clyde R. "Israel's Security Fences, Separating Israel from the Palestinians", CRS Report for Congress (1 August 2003), CRS-2, https://digital.library.unt.edu/ark:/67531/metacrs7718/m1/1/high_res_d/RS21564_2003Aug01.pdf

McDuie-Ra, Duncan. "Tribals, Migrants and Insurgents: Security and Insecurity along the India-Bangladesh Border", *Global Change, Peace & Security*, Vol. 24, No. 1 (2012), pp. 165–82, https://doi.org/10.1080/14781158.2012.641286

McElroy, Damien. "Tashkent Urged to Allow UN Aid Across Bridge", *The Daily Telegraph* (11 November 2001), http://www.telegraph.co.uk/news/worldnews/asia/uzbekistan/1362221/Tashkent-urged-to-allow-UN-aid-across-bridge.html

Megoran, Nick. "The Critical Geopolitics of the Uzbekistan-Kyrgyzstan Ferghana Valley Boundary Dispute, 1999–2000", *Political Geography*, Vol. 23, No. 6 (2004), pp. 731–64, https://doi.org/10.1016/j.polgeo.2004.03.004

Megoran, Nick. "Rethinking the Study of International Boundaries: A Biography of the Kyrgyzstan-Uzbekistan Boundary", *Annals of the Association of American Geographers*, Vol. 102, No. 2 (2012), pp. 464–81, https://doi.org/10.1080/00045608.2011.595969

Mehrotra-Khanna, Mansi. "Security Challenges to India-Bangladesh Relations", working paper series 1, Center for Land Warfare Studies (2010).

Messari, Mohamed Larbi. "The Vivid Memories of Al-Andalus in the Discourse on Dialogue among Civilisations" (2006).

Messari, Mohamed Larbi. "The Current Context of a Moroccan Claim to Ceuta and Melilla", *Dafatir Siyassiya*, No. 107 (December 2009) [in Arabic].

Migdalovitz, Carol. "Israel: Background and Relations with the United States", *Congressional Research Service* (2 April 2009), p. 19.

Migration and Remittances Factbook 2016 — 3rd edition. Washington: The World Bank Group, 2016, https://openknowledge.worldbank.org/bitstream/handle/10986/23743/9781464803192.pdf

Misuse of Licit Trade for Opiate Trafficking in Western and Central Asia: A Threat Assessment. UNODC (October 2012).

Mitnick, Joshua. "Israel Finishes Most of Fence on Sinai Border", *The Wall Street Journal* (2 January 2013), http://online.wsj.com/article/SB10001424127887324374004578217720772159626.html

Mohsen-Finan, Khadija. "Murs de Défense au Sahara Occidental", *Études*, Vol. 400, No. 2004 (January 2004), p. 94.

Moniquet, Claude. "The POLISARIO Front: Credible Negotiations Partner or After-Effect of the Cold War and Obstacle to a Political Solution in Western Sahara?" *European Strategic Intelligence & Security Center (ESISC)* (November 2005).

Myntti, Kristian. "The Beneficiaries of Autonomy Arrangements — with Special Reference to Indigenous Peoples in General and the Saami in Finland in Particular", in *Autonomy: Applications and Implications*, Markku Suksi (Ed.). The Hague: Kluwer Law International, 1998, pp. 277–94.

Nallu, Preethi. "Europe's Refugee Frontier: Pushbacks and Border Closures in Serbia", News Daily (24 March 2017), https://www.newsdeeply.com/refugees/articles/2017/03/24/europes-refugee-frontier-pushbacks-and-border-closures-in-serbia-2

"National Border Patrol Strategy" Department of Homeland Security, Bureau of Customs and Border Protection (1 March 2005).

Neill, Alexander. "Towards Cross-Border Security", Occasional Paper, Royal United Services Institute (February 2010).

Nelson, Rick "Ozzie". "Border Security in a Time of Transformation: Two International Case Studies — Poland and India", A Report of the CSIS Homeland Security & Counterterrorism Program, Europe Program, and South Asia Program (July 2010), http://csis.org/files/publication/100709_Nelson_BorderSecurity_web.pdf

Nevins, Joseph. "'Illegal Aliens' and the Political Geography of Criminalized Immigrants", paper presented at the annual meeting of the Association of American Geographers, Boston, U.S. (8 March 1998).

"No Man's Land in M'sia-Thai Border to be Scrapped", *Utusan Malaysia Internet Edition* (3 August 2001), http://ww1.utusan.com.my/utusan/info.asp?y=2001&dt=0803&pub=Utusan_Express&sec=Home_News&pg=hn_08.htm

Norton, Augustus Richard and Jillian Schwedler. "(In)security Zones in South Lebanon", *Journal of Palestine Studies*, Vol. 23, No. 1 (1993), pp. 61–79, https://doi.org/10.2307/2537858

Novosseloff, Alexandra, and Frank Neisse. "La construction des murs, ou la mondialisation à rebours", *Questions internationales*, No. 33 (September-October 2008), p. 101.

Ohmae, Kenichi. *The Borderless World: Power and Strategy in the Interlinked Economy*. New York: Harper Business, 1999.

O'Reilly, Gerry. *Ceuta and the Spanish Sovereign Territories: Spanish and Moroccan Claims*. Durham: International Boundaries Research Unit, Dept. of Geography, University of Durham (1994).

PLO Negotiations Affairs Department, "Bad Fences Make Bad Neighbors", *The Palestine-Israel Journal*, Vol. 9, No. 3 (2002), http://www.pij.org/details.php?id=140

Passel, Jeffrey S. and D'Vera Cohn. "U.S. Unauthorized Immigration Flows are Down Sharply since Mid-Decade", *The Pew Hispanic Center* (1 September 2010).

Pattanaik, Smruti S. "India-Bangladesh Land Border: A Flawed Inheritance and a Problematic Future", *Strategic Analysis*, Vol. 35, No. 5 (2011), pp. 745–75, https://doi.org/10.1080/09700161.2011.591763

Pinos, Jaume Castan. "Identity Challenges affecting the Spanish Enclaves of Ceuta and Melilla", *Nordlit*, No. 24 (2009), pp. 65–80.

Pinyol, Gemma. "The External Dimension of the European Immigration Policy: A Spanish Perspective", paper presented at the conference "The Euro-Mediterranean Partnership (EMP): Perspectives from the Mediterranean EU Countries", Rethymnon, Crete (25–27 October 2007).

Policy Plan on Legal Migration. Commission of the European Communities (2005) 669 (21 December 2005), http://eur-lex.europa.eu/legal-content/EN/TXT/?uri=COM:2005:0669:FIN

"Population and Housing Census 2011: Socio-economic and Demographic Report", Bangladesh Bureau of Statistics (BBS), Statistics and Informatics Division (SID), Ministry of Planning, National Series, Vol. 4 (December 2012), http://203.112.218.66/WebTestApplication/userfiles/Image/BBS/Socio_Economic.pdf

Qojas, Mazen. "Cooperative Border Security for Jordan: Assessment and Options", *Cooperative Monitoring Center Occasional Papers/8* (March 1999), http://www.sandia.gov/cooperative-monitoring-center/_assets/documents/sand98-05058.pdf

Qureshi, S. M. M. "Pakhtunistan: The Frontier Dispute between Afghanistan and Pakistan", *Pacific Affairs*, Vol. 39, No. 1/2 (1966), pp. 99–114, https://doi.org/10.2307/2755184

Ramachandran, Sudha. "India: No Sitting on the Fence", *Asia Times Online* (3 December 2003), http://www.atimes.com/atimes/South_Asia/EL03Df05.html

Rashid, Harun Ur. *Indo-Bangladesh Relations: An Insider's View*. New Delhi: Har-Anand Publications, 2002.

Rashid, Harun Ur. "Syria Calls on UN to Thwart Israel's 'Separation Fence' on Golan Heights", *Haaretz* (15 August 2011), http://www.haaretz.com/syria-calls-on-un-to-thwart-israel-s-separation-fence-on-golan-heights-1.378642

Ravid, Barak. "Israel to Build NIS 1.5b Fence along Egypt Border", *Haaretz* (1 October 2010), http://www.haaretz.com/israel-to-build-nis-1-5b-fence-along-egypt-border-1.261141

Rezette, Robert. *The Spanish Enclaves in Morocco*. Paris: Nouvelles Editions Latines, 1976.

Richardson, Michael. "Malaysia Border-Wall Plan Strains Thailand Ties", *The New York Times* (10 July 1991).

Ritaine, Évelyne. "La Barrière et le Checkpoint: Mise en Politique de L'asymétrie", *Cultures & Conflits*, No. 73 (2009), pp. 15–33, https://doi.org/10.4000/conflits.17500

Rosenau, James N. "New Dimensions of Security: The Interaction of Globalizing the Localizing Dynamics", *Security Dialogue*, Vol. 25, No. 3 (1994), pp. 255–82, http://journals.sagepub.com/doi/abs/10.1177/0967010694025003003

Rosenberg, Mica and Jonathan Stempel. "U.S. Judges Limit Trump Immigration Order; Some Officials Ignore Rulings", *Reuters* (29 January 2017), http://www.reuters.com/article/us-usa-trump-immigration-courts-idUSKBN15D0XG

Rotstein, Arthur H.. "Officials Ready to Build Virtual Fence along Border", *USnews & World Report* (8 May 2009), http://www.usnews.com/science/articles/2009/05/08/officials-ready-to-build-virtual-fence-along-border

Saada, Julien. "L'économie du Mur: Un Marché en Pleine Expansion", *Le Devoir* (27 October 2009), http://www.ledevoir.com/international/actualites-internationales/271687/l-economie-du-mur-un-marche-en-pleine-expansion

Saddiki, Said. "A Reading of the Constitution 'Sahrawi Arab Democratic Republic", *Southern Morocco News Letter* (2008), pp. 77–92.

Saddiki, Said. "The International Reference of the Moroccan Autonomy Project for the Sahara Region", *Southern Morocco News Letter* (July 2008), pp. 15–25.

Saddiki, Said. "El papel de la diplomacia cultural en las relaciones internacionales", *Revista CIDOB d'Afers Internacionals*, No. 88 (December 2009), pp. 107–18, http://www.raco.cat/index.php/RevistaCIDOB/article/view/164488/216461

Saddiki, Said. "Les Clôtures de Ceuta et de Melilla: Une Frontière Européenne Multidimensionnelle", *Études internationales*, Vol. 43, No. 1 (2012), pp. 49–65.

Saddiki, Said. "Israel and the Fencing Policy: A Barrier on Every Seam Line", research paper, Arab Center for Research and Policy Studies (June 2015).

Saikia, Pradip. "North-East India as a Factor in India's Diplomatic Engagement with Myanmar: Issues and Challenges", *Strategic Analysis*, Vol. 33, No. 6 (2009), pp. 877–89, https://doi.org/10.1080/09700160903255889

Schendel, Willem van. *The Bengal Borderland: Beyond State and Nation in South Asia*. London: Anthem Press, 2005.

Schofield, Clive H. "Elusive Security: The Military and Political Geography of South Lebanon", *GeoJournal*, Vol. 31, No. 2 (1993), pp. 149–62, https://doi.org/10.1007/bf00808687

Scott, James Brown. "The Swiss Decision in the Boundary Dispute between Colombia and Venezuela", *American Journal of International Law*, Vol. 16, No. 3 (1922), pp. 428–31, https://doi.org/10.2307/2188181

Secure Border Initiative Fence Construction Costs, United States Government Accountability Office [Washington, D.C.] (29 January 2009), http://www.gao.gov/products/GAO-09-244R

"Secure Border Initiative: DHS Needs to Strengthen Management and Oversight of Its Prime Contractor", Report to Congressional Requesters, United States Government Accountability Office (October 2010), http://www.gao.gov/assets/320/311441.pdf

"Securing the Wall from International Law: An Initial Response to the Israeli State Attorney", position paper Palestinian Centre for Human Rights (April 2005).

Sengupta, Anita. "Afghan Watershed for Central Asia", *Economic and Political Weekly*, Vol. 36, No. 42 (2001), pp. 3985–7.

Shamshad, Rizwana. "Politics and Origin of the Indian-Bangladesh Border Fence", paper presented to the 17th Biennial Conference of the Asian Studies Association of Australia, Melbourne (1–3 July 2008).

Sharp, Jeremy. "The Egypt-Gaza Border and its Effect on Israeli-Egyptian Relations", Congressional Research Service, Report No. RL34346 (1 February 2008), http://www.fas.org/sgp/crs/mideast/RL34346.pdf

Shazli, Sa'ad Din. "How the Egyptians Crossed the Canal", *Journal of Palestine Studies*, Vol. 3, No. 2 (1974), pp. 163–8, https://doi.org/10.2307/2535814

Shields, Peter. "ICTs and the European Union's Evolving Border Surveillance Architecture: A Critical Assessment", *Observatorio (OBS*) Journal*, Vol. 4, No. 1 (2010), pp. 255–88.

Singh, Langpoklakpam Suraj. "Indo-Myanmar Relations in the Greater Perspective of India's Look East Policy: Implications on Manipur", in *Look East Policy & India's North East: Polemics and Perspectives*, Thingnam Kishan Singh (Ed.). New Delhi: Concept, 2008.

Singh, Ravinder. "Fencing and Floodlighting for Better Vigil along Borders", *The Indian Post Daily News* (10 February 2010), http://www.theindiapost. com/articles/fencing-and-floodlighting-for-better-vigil-along-borders/

"Special Report. Egyptian Government Infected by Mad Israeli Wall Disease", Arab Organization for Human Rights in the UK (AOHR) (30 December 2009).

Strengthening Afghan-Iran Drug Border Control and Cross Border Cooperation (SAID). Project Number: AFG/H16, Vienna, UNODC (May 2009).

Suksi, Markku. "On the Entrenchment of Autonomy", in *Autonomy: Applications and Implications*, Markku Suksi (Ed.). The Hague: Kluwer Law International, 1998.

Swami, Praveen. "Failed Threats and Flawed Fences: India's Military Responses to Pakistan's Proxy War", *India Review*, Vol. 3, No. 2 (2004), pp. 147–70, https://doi.org/10.1080/14736480490465045

Taksanov, Alisher. "Policy Use of Antipersonnel Mines in Uzbekistan, 2004", http://fr.scribd.com/doc/95916900/Policy-use-of-antipersonnel-mines-in-Uzbekistan-2004

"Technical Mission to Morocco. Visit to Ceuta and Melilla on Illegal Immigration", Mission Report, European Commission (7–11October 2005), http://www. migreurop.org/IMG/pdf/rapport-ceuta-melilla-2.pdf

"Thailand and Malaysia Agree to Lengthen Border Security Wall", *German Press Agency* (14 February 2007), http://rawstory.com/news/2007/Thailand_and_ Malaysia_agree_to_leng_02142007.html

"The Immigration in an Interconnected World: New Directions for Action", Global Commission on International Immigration (October 2005).

"The Impact of Israel's Separation Barrier on Affected West Bank Communities", The Humanitarian and Emergency Policy Group and the Local Aid Coordination Committee (4 May 2003), http://www.hamoked.org/ files/2011/3540_eng.pdf

"The Israeli Apartheid Separation Wall to Control the Palestinian Water Resources", report prepared by the PWA in cooperation with Sustainable Management of the West Bank and Gaza Aquifer, Palestinian National Authority and PWA (5 February 2003).

"The Israeli Racist Separation Wall: Consequences and Violations" Palestinian National Authority, State Information Center (10 October 2003), http://w3.osa archivum.org/galeria/the_divide/cpt14files/the_israeli_racist_separation_ wall.doc

Thornberry, Patrick. "The Democratic or Internal Aspect of Self-determination with Some Remarks on Federalism", in *Modern Law of Self-Determination*, Christian Tomuschat (Ed.). Dordrecht: Martinus Nijhoff, 1993, pp. 101–38.

Tinker, Hugh. *India and Pakistan: A Short Political Guide*. London: Pall Mall Press, 1962.

Towards a Fair Deal for Migrant Workers in the Global Economy, International Labour Conference, 92nd Session. Geneva: International Labour Office, 2004.

Trottier, Julie, "A Wall, Water and Power: The Israeli 'Separation Fence'", *Review of International Studies*, Vol. 33, No. 1 (2007), pp. 105–27, https://doi.org/10.1017/s0260210507007334

"UNODC Director Praises Iran's Drug Control Efforts, Calls for Greater International Support", press release, United Nations Office on Drugs and Crime (20 May 2009), http://www.unodc.org/unodc/en/press/releases/2009/May/2009-19.05.html

Vallet, Élisabeth and Charles-Philippe David. "Introduction. Du Retour des Murs Frontaliers en Relations Internationales", *Études Internationales*, Vol. 43, no. 1 (2012), pp. 5–25, https://doi.org/10.7202/1009137ar

Vallet, Élisabeth. "Toujours Plus de Murs dans un Monde sans Frontières", *Le Devoir* (26 October 2009), http://www.ledevoir.com/international/actualites-internationales/273594/toujours-plus-de-murs-dans-un-monde-sans-frontieres

Venter, Al J. "Israel Last Line of Defense", *Jane's International Defense Review*, Vol. 29 No. 11 (1996), pp. 59–61.

Vinayaraj, V. K. "India as a Threat: Bangladesh Perceptions", *South Asian Survey*, Vol. 16, No. 1 (2009), pp. 101–18, https://doi.org/10.1177/097152310801600107

Vinokurov, Evgeny. *A Theory of Enclaves*. Lanham: Lexington Books, 2007.

Waslin, Michele. "The New Meaning of the Border: U.S.-Mexico Migration Since 9/11", paper prepared for the conference on "Reforming the Administration of Justice in Mexico", the Center for U.S.-Mexican Studies, University of California [San Diego] (15–17 May 2003), http://escholarship.org/uc/item/3dd8w0r6

Worden, Tom. "Spain Sees Sixfold Increase in Immigrants over Decade", *The Guardian* (8 February 2010), https://www.theguardian.com/world/2010/feb/08/spain-sixfold-increase-immigrants

World Drug Report 2010. Vienna: United Nations Publication, 2010, https://www.unodc.org/documents/wdr/WDR_2010/World_Drug_Report_2010_lo-res.pdf

World Drug Report 2011. New York: United Nations Publication, 2011, https://www.unodc.org/unodc/en/data-and-analysis/WDR-2011.html

World Migration Report 2010: The Future of Migration: Building Capacities for Change. Geneva, Switzerland: IOM, 2010, https://publications.iom.int/system/files/pdf/wmr_2010_english.pdf

World Migration Report 2008: *Managing Labor Mobility in the Evolving Global Economy*. Geneva, Switzerland: IOM, 2008, https://publications.iom.int/books/world-migration-report-2008-managing-labour-mobility-evolving-global-economy

Zapata-Barrero, Ricard and Nynke De Witte. "Spain", in *EU and US Approaches to the Management of Immigration*: *Comparative Perspectives*, J. Niessen and Y. Schibel (Ed.). Brussels: Migration Policy Group, 2003, http://www.migpolgroup.com/public/docs/143.Spain_EU-USapproachestotheManagem entofImmigration_2003.pdf

Zapata-Barrero, Ricard and Nynke De Witte. "The Spanish Governance of EU Borders: Normative Questions", *Mediterranean Politics*, Vol. 12, No. 1 (2007), pp. 85–90, https://doi.org/10.1080/13629390601136863

Zapata-Barrero, Ricard and Nynke De Witte. "Perceptions and Realities of Moroccan Immigration Flows and Spanish Policies". *Journal of Immigrant & Refugee Studies* Vol. 6, No. 3 (2008), pp. 382–96, https://doi.org/10.1080/15362940802371697

Zartman, William. *Ripe for Resolution: Conflict and Intervention in Africa*. New York: Oxford University Press, 1989.

Index

This book need not end here…

At Open Book Publishers, we are changing the nature of the traditional academic book. The title you have just read will not be left on a library shelf, but will be accessed online by hundreds of readers each month across the globe. OBP publishes only the best academic work: each title passes through a rigorous peer-review process. We make all our books free to read online so that students, researchers and members of the public who can't afford a printed edition will have access to the same ideas.
This book and additional content is available at:
https://www.openbookpublishers.com/product/635

Customize

Personalize your copy of this book or design new books using OBP and third-party material. Take chapters or whole books from our published list and make a special edition, a new anthology or an illuminating coursepack. Each customized edition will be produced as a paperback and a downloadable PDF. Find out more at:
https://www.openbookpublishers.com/section/59/1

Donate

If you enjoyed this book, and feel that research like this should be available to all readers, regardless of their income, please think about donating to us. We do not operate for profit and all donations, as with all other revenue we generate, will be used to finance new Open Access publications.
https://www.openbookpublishers.com/section/13/1/support-us

f   Like Open Book Publishers

🐦   Follow @OpenBookPublish

BLOG   Read more at the OBP Blog

You may also be interested in:

Frontier Encounters
Knowledge and Practice at the Russian, Chinese and Mongolian Border

Edited by Franck Billé, Grégory Delaplace and Caroline Humphrey

https://www.openbookpublishers.com/product/139

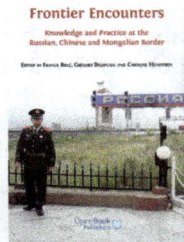

Peace and Democratic Society

Edited by Amartya Sen

https://www.openbookpublishers.com/product/78

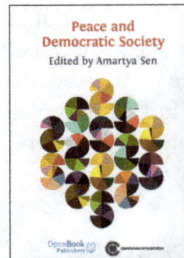

The Universal Declaration of Human Rights
in the 21st Century

Edited by Gordon Brown

https://www.openbookpublishers.com/product/467